THE FIRST WORLD WAR

For four long years the nightmare lasted in Europe. The number of men who put their lives at risk without really knowing why was infinite. Prosperous lands were plunged into poverty... Old countries were swept away and new ones appeared in their place. This was the age of the Great War, more costly and more destructive than any other previous conflict. Many believed that this struggle would forever put an end to war! But that was a miscalculation...
This was not the last war, but the First World War!

THE ASSASSINATION

In 1914, Austria was an empire which housed a number of minority groups such as the Serbs, Bohemians and Hungarians. These people were hostile to the Austrian government. The Serbs in particular were striving for independence. They wanted their territory to be united with the neighbouring Kingdom of Serbia.

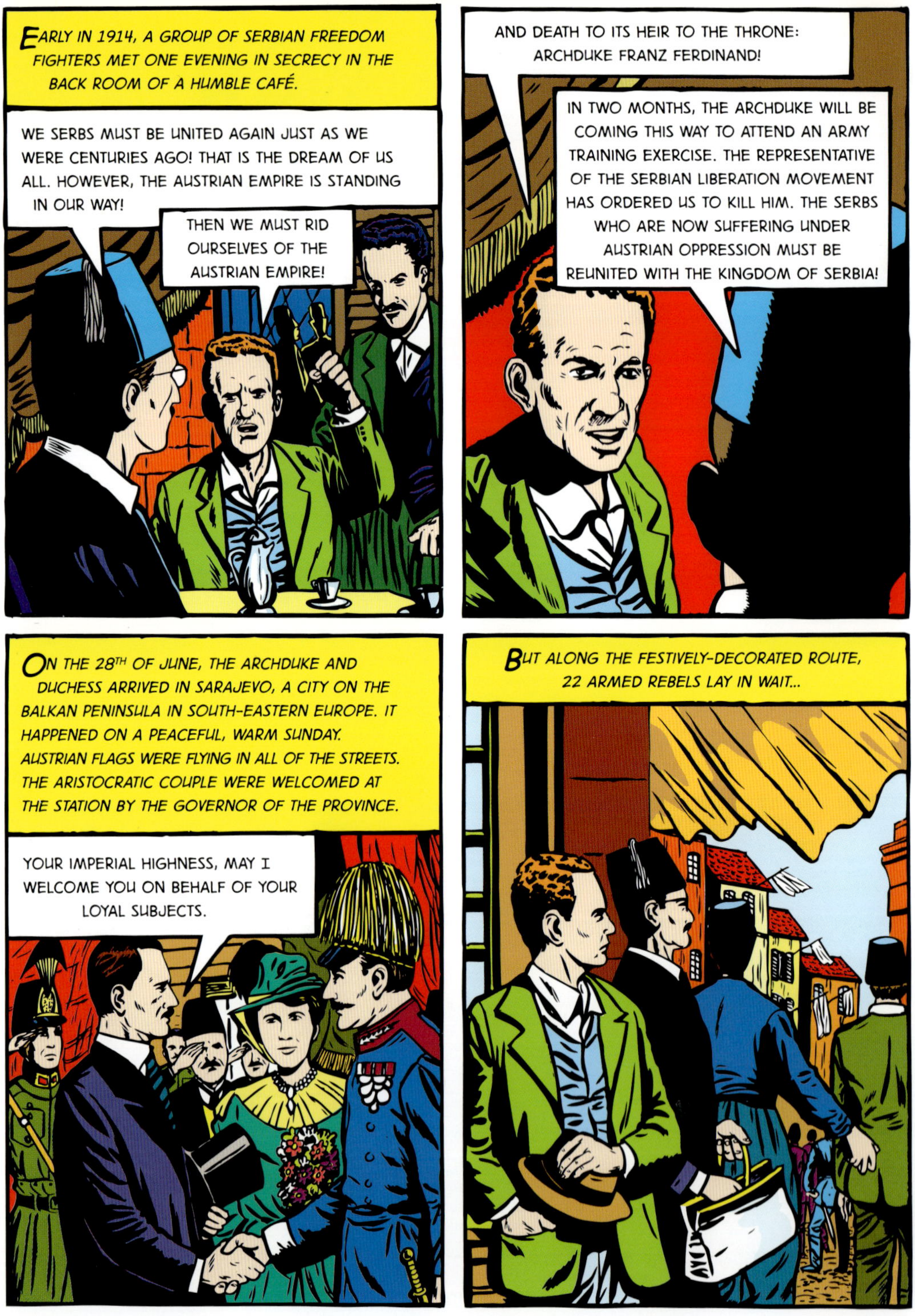

Archduke Franz Ferdinand had been warned against visiting the Balkans. However, he refused to cancel the visit, and wore a bullet-proof vest under his uniform. When the procession had driven away from the station, someone threw a bomb at the Archduke's car.

Remarkably, he reached Sarajevo town hall unhurt.

LORD MAYOR, I COME HERE WITH FRIENDLY INTENTIONS, BUT I AM GREETED WITH A BOMB! WHAT IS THE MEANING OF THIS?

After an official reception at the town hall, the royal guests continued their drive along the main street of the city...

YOUR IMPERIAL HIGHNESS, YOU ARE NOW PERFECTLY SAFE! I KNOW MY PEOPLE! THEY WOULD NEVER ATTACK YOU TWICE IN THE SAME DAY!

Suddenly two shots rang out...

SOPHIE! SOPHIE! WHAT ON EARTH IS HAPPENING?!

The shots had found their target! Archduke Franz Ferdinand, heir to the Austrian Empire, was dead.

Anti-Serbian demonstrations now broke out in the Austrian capital, Vienna...	**Austria wanted to take punitive measures against the Serbian kingdom and to do this, they sought help from neighbouring Germany.**
"To the Serbian embassy!"	"Franz Ferdinand has been assassinated by Serbian agents! That country must be wiped off the map for good!"
"Oafish rabble! There's always trouble with the Balkans... but it'll die down!"	"Act as you see fit! Germany is behind you!"

Panel 3	Panel 4	Panel 5
One month after the attack, Austria sent Serbia a list of stringent demands. If the Serbian government did not surrender within 48 hours, Austria would declare war on Serbia.	**Serbia was unable to accept the ultimatum and preserve her independence, so she refused, and on the 28th of July came the Austrian declaration of war.**	**In the summer of 1914, everyone began to wonder if the Balkan war would spread...**
"Serbia will never comply with our demands, but that is what we want! We will then have an excuse to attack!"		"The international situation has widened alarmingly."
		"Yes, it's likely that this will develop into an all-out war. Everything now depends on Germany."

BLOOD AND IRON

Before the mid-nineteenth century, Germany was made up of a large number of small independent states. The largest of these, Prussia, united these states into one strong nation.

Chancellor Otto von Bismarck made the German army the strongest in Europe. He instilled Prussian discipline into the whole of Germany.

*There is only one solution to the great problems of today's world: **BLOOD AND IRON!***

During the nineteenth century, Germany revealed her might in a variety of minor wars. After her victory over France in 1870, Germany was feared and mistrusted by almost all her neighbours.

It's awful! Germany conquers France in just a few months and also eyes up a couple of our provinces!

We haven't seen the last of the Germans! There will come a time when we will have to give them back Alsace and Lorraine!

In 1882, a new German emperor was crowned...

Your Majesty is no doubt right. We must build a colonial empire. Germany has a right to the same wealth as France and England!

If not more! I shall rule over the greatest empire in the world! And the new German navy will bring this about!

But there were also other European countries seeking wealth via the acquisition of colonial power...

Germany is a danger to us! We must show who rules the waves! Britain must have more warships!

5

There followed a great arms race. Each country claimed to be acting in self-defence. No one state wished to be seen as weak. The great powers of Europe had but one objective... to be in possession of the greatest, strongest and most destructive military might!

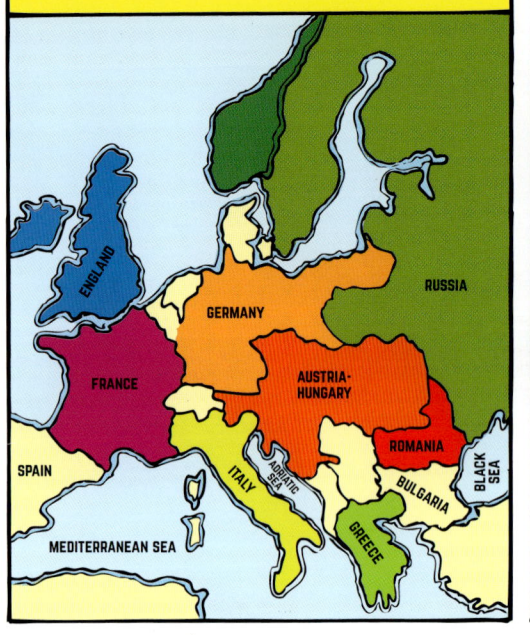

Since none of those countries was a match for the others on its own, many of them drew up military alliances. Germany took sides with Italy and Austria.

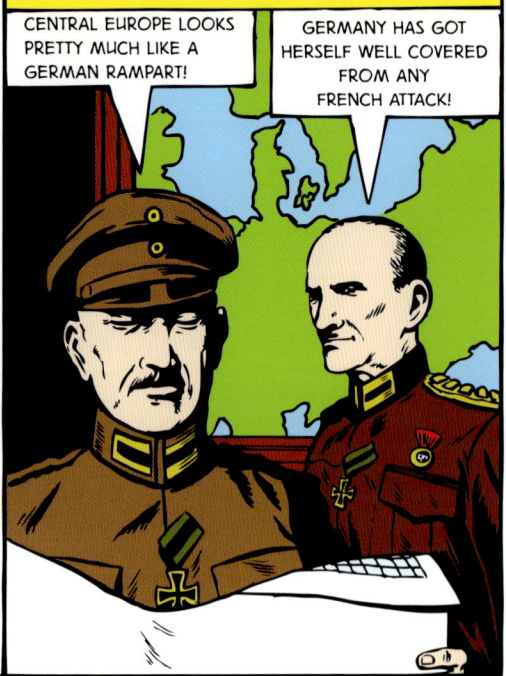

"Central Europe looks pretty much like a German rampart!"

"Germany has got herself well covered from any French attack!"

But France responded with an alliance with Russia...

"Gentlemen, we've now got Germany surrounded. She will definitely not launch a war against two fronts simultaneously!"

A few smaller countries sought protection through treaties with the great powers.

"Russia will guarantee the safety of Serbia if Britain does likewise with Belgium."

Some countries kept their treaties a secret. This was often met with resistance, but the Europeans were proud of their national military power!

"The government has betrayed you! You might be giving up your lives for a couple of dead aristocrats."

"That fellow is insulting the honour of our country! Down with the traitor!"

AROUND 1907, THE GREATEST POWERS IN EUROPE HAD DIVIDED THEMSELVES INTO TWO FACTIONS, BOTH ARMED-TO-THE-TEETH. FRANCE AND HER ALLIES WERE KNOWN AS THE TRIPLE ENTENTE AND GERMANY, UNITED WITH OTHER COUNTRIES, AS THE TRIPLE ALLIANCE. THE TWO SIDES WERE FREQUENTLY IN DISPUTE, THOUGH TIME AND AGAIN ARMED CONFLICT WAS AVOIDED. BUT TENSION WAS MOUNTING...

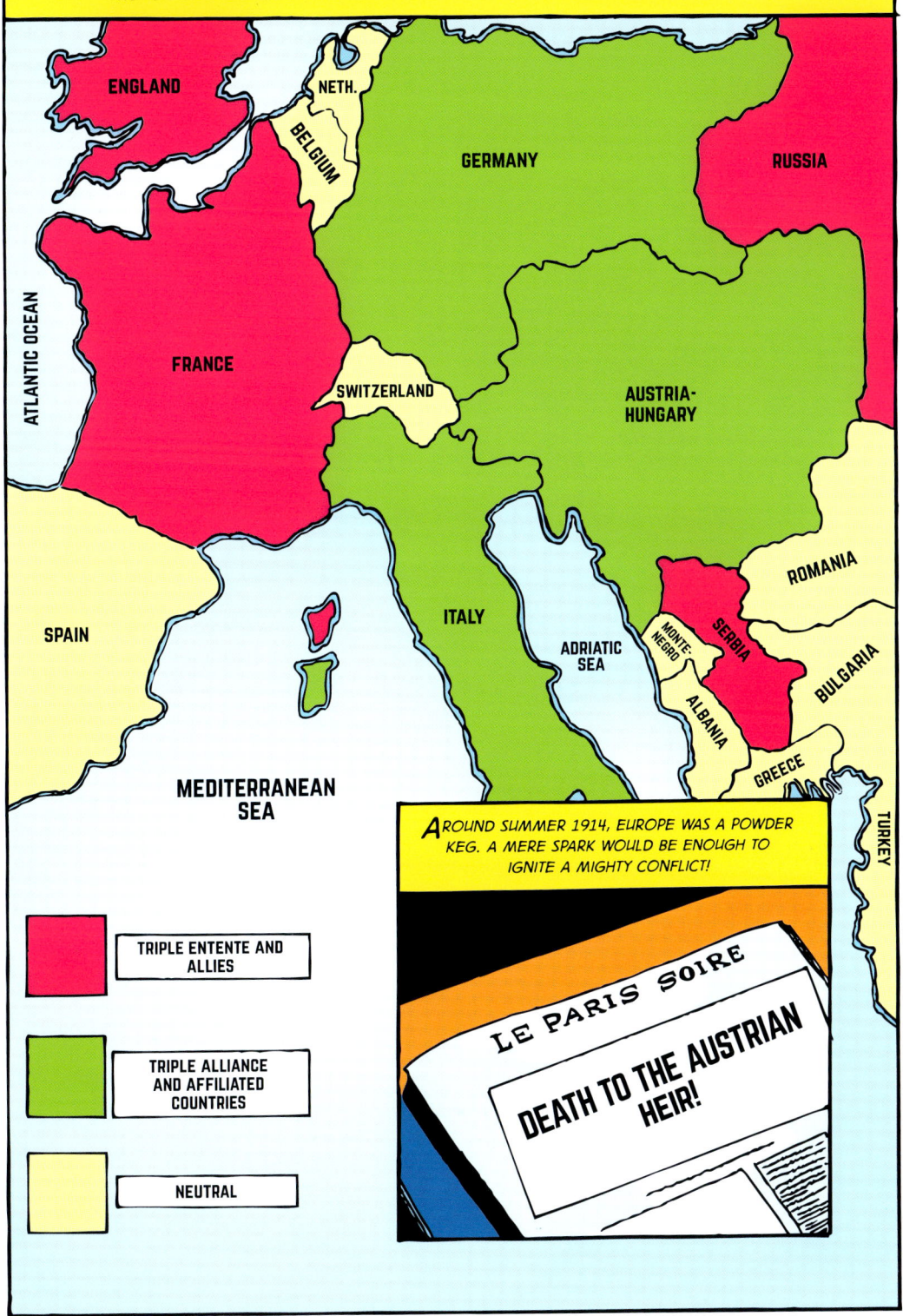

Color	Meaning
Red	TRIPLE ENTENTE AND ALLIES
Green	TRIPLE ALLIANCE AND AFFILIATED COUNTRIES
Yellow	NEUTRAL

AROUND SUMMER 1914, EUROPE WAS A POWDER KEG. A MERE SPARK WOULD BE ENOUGH TO IGNITE A MIGHTY CONFLICT!

LE PARIS SOIRE

DEATH TO THE AUSTRIAN HEIR!

CHAIN REACTIONS

WITHIN A WEEK OF THE AUSTRIAN DECLARATION OF WAR, THE EUROPEAN ALLIES BECAME INVOLVED IN THE CONFLICT ONE AFTER ANOTHER!

ON THE 29TH OF JULY, RUSSIA SENT TROOPS TO THE AUSTRIAN BORDER TO HELP THE SERBS.

THE GERMAN GOVERNMENT WILL NEGOTIATE IF WE WITHDRAW OUR TROOPS WITHIN TWELVE HOURS.

IMPOSSIBLE! OUR PREPARATIONS HAVE GONE TOO FAR!

THE FOLLOWING DAY, AUSTRIA, GERMANY AND FRANCE MOBILISED THEIR ARMIES...

THE GERMAN GOVERNMENT WISHES FRANCE TO REMAIN NEUTRAL IF GERMANY BEGINS A CAMPAIGN AGAINST RUSSIA!

WE CANNOT GUARANTEE THAT. IN THE FIRST INSTANCE, FRANCE WILL BE MOTIVATED BY HER OWN INTERESTS.

WHEN RUSSIA FAILED TO ANSWER THE ULTIMATUM, THE GERMAN ARMY SWUNG INTO ACTION...

WE'LL TEACH THE RUSSIANS SOME MANNERS!

AND SO THE CHANCE TO NEGOTIATE A LASTING PEACE WAS GONE.

FRANCE IS GOING TO HELP THE RUSSIANS. WE DON'T WAIT FOR THEM TO ATTACK US FROM BEHIND. GERMANY MUST DECLARE WAR ON FRANCE!

THE SHORTEST ROUTE FOR A GERMAN ATTACK ON FRANCE LAY THROUGH BELGIUM, WHICH WAS NEUTRAL. BELGIUM REFUSED TO LET GERMAN TROOPS THROUGH. ON THE 3RD AND 4TH OF AUGUST, HOWEVER, SHE WAS OVERRUN BY THE GERMANS. BRITAIN COULD NOT LET SUCH A VIOLATION OF NEUTRALITY GO BY UNCHALLENGED.

ON THE 4TH OF AUGUST, THE GOVERNMENT IN LONDON ORDERED THE GERMANS TO CALL OFF THEIR ATTACK WITHIN 6 HOURS. THE GERMANS REFUSED.

OUR ALLIANCE WITH BELGIUM COMPELS US TO DEFEND THE NEUTRALITY OF THAT COUNTRY. I THEREFORE ASK THE HOUSE TO SUPPORT A DECLARATION OF WAR BY HIS MAJESTY'S GOVERNMENT AGAINST THE GERMAN EMPIRE!

AND SO THE GREAT WAR BECAME REALITY! OF THE GREAT EUROPEAN POWERS, ONLY ITALY REMAINED NEUTRAL. THE BRITISH FOREIGN SECRETARY, SIR EDWARD GREY, ON THE EVENING OF HIS COUNTRY'S DECLARATION OF WAR, SUMMED UP THE THOUGHTS OF THE WHOLE WORLD...

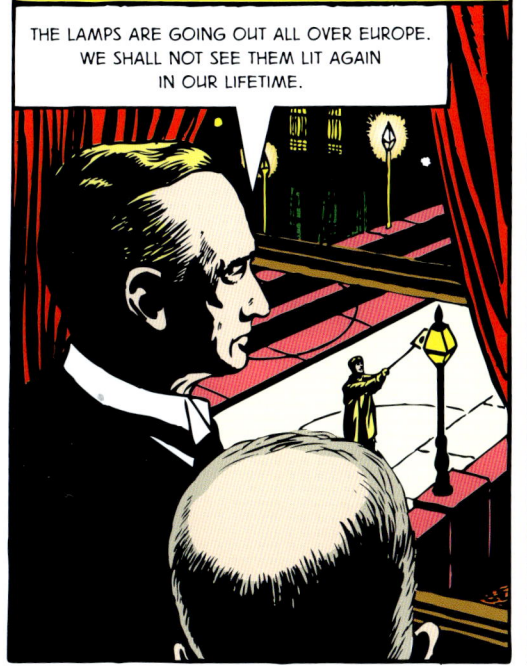

THE LAMPS ARE GOING OUT ALL OVER EUROPE. WE SHALL NOT SEE THEM LIT AGAIN IN OUR LIFETIME.

MORE THAN 20 OTHER NATIONS SUBSEQUENTLY JOINED IN THE WAR. THE QUARREL BETWEEN RUSSIA AND SERBIA AND THE ASSASSINATION OF THE ARCHDUKE FADED INTO OBLIVION. ALL EYES TURNED TOWARDS THE STRUGGLE BETWEEN GERMANY AND FRANCE... AND ON WHAT BECAME KNOWN AS THE WESTERN FRONT.

Y NEEDS YOU

DEATH TO THE AUSTRIAN SUCCESSOR

THE INVASION OF BELGIUM

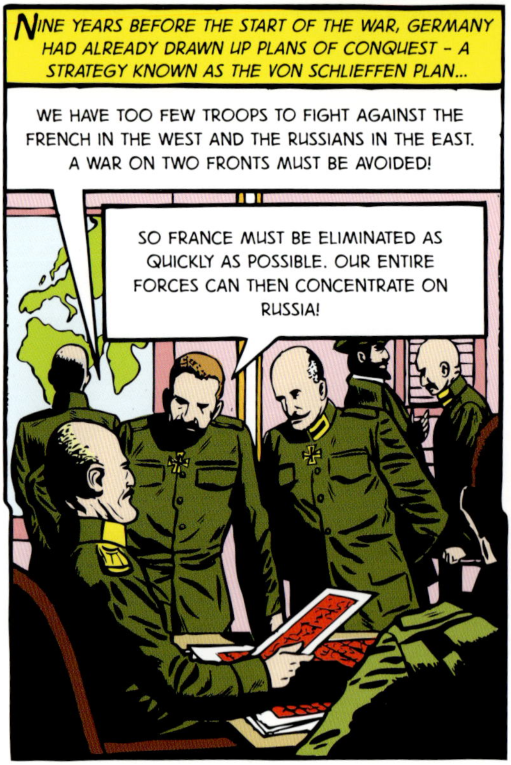

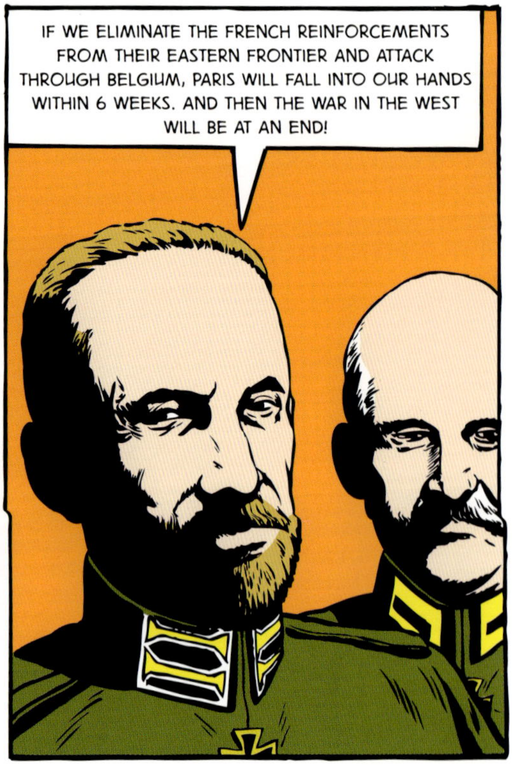

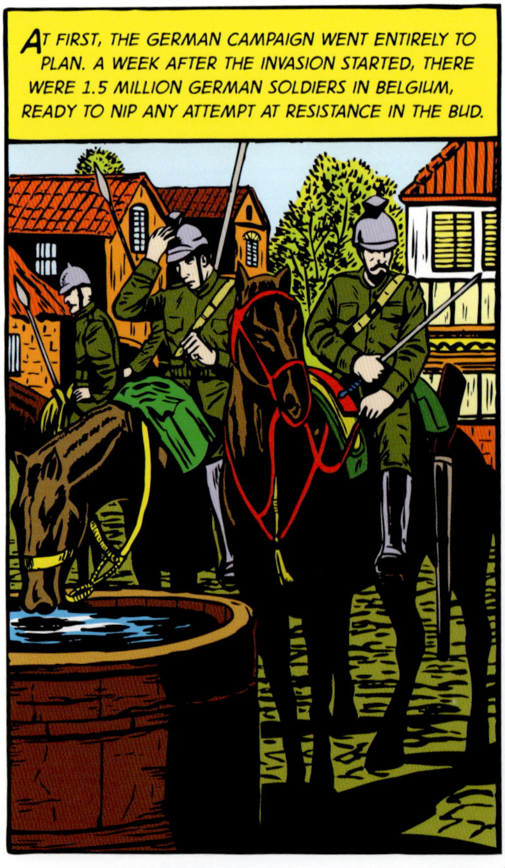

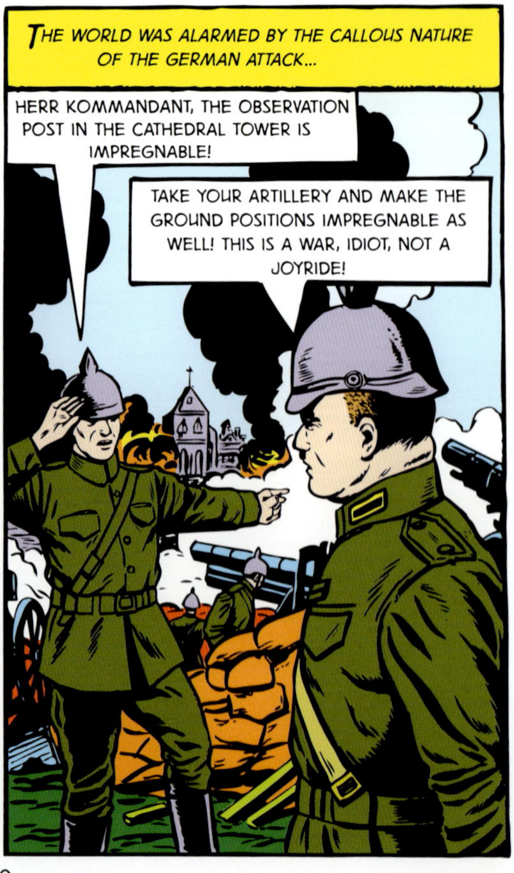

BELGIUM WAS NOT PREPARED FOR WAR. THE SMALL BELGIAN ARMY PUT UP STUBBORN RESISTANCE, BUT ON THE 5TH OF AUGUST IT WAS PUSHED BACK TO THE FORTIFIED TOWN OF LIÈGE.

LIÈGE LAY RIGHT ALONG THE ROUTE WHICH THE GERMANS FOLLOWED IN A SOUTH-WESTERLY DIRECTION TOWARDS THE NORTHERN FRENCH BORDER. GERMAN TROOPS STORMED THE OPEN GROUND BETWEEN THE TWELVE FORTIFICATIONS MEANT TO PROTECT THE TOWN. THE BELGIAN INFANTRY MET THEM WITH RIFLES AND BAYONETS. THE GERMANS WERE BEATEN BACK...

THAT SAME NIGHT, A GERMAN GENERAL, ERICH LUDENDORFF, PERSONALLY LED HIS TROOPS BETWEEN TWO FORTIFICATIONS DEEP INTO THE TOWN.

"YOU ARE HEAVILY OUTNUMBERED! IF YOU DO NOT SURRENDER, WE SHALL RAZE THIS TOWN TO THE GROUND!"

LIÈGE SURRENDERED... BUT IN THE FORTIFICATIONS THE FIGHT CARRIED ON. THE GERMANS QUIETLY MOVED THEIR HEAVY CANNONS IN... THEIR BOMBARDMENT LASTED ALL NIGHT. BY MORNING, THE LIÈGE FORTIFICATIONS HAD BEEN ERADICATED.

THE BELGIAN PEOPLE MOSTLY FLED SOUTH TO KEEP OUT OF THE CLUTCHES OF THE INVADERS.

ON THE 18TH OF AUGUST, THE LAST FORTIFICATION FELL IN LIÈGE. THE BELGIAN ARMY RETREATED TO THE PORT OF ANTWERP, 110 KILOMETRES NORTH-WEST.

BRUSSELS, THE CAPITAL OF BELGIUM, FELL INTO GERMAN HANDS TWO DAYS LATER. THE ATTACKING ARMIES ADVANCED SWIFTLY TOWARDS FRANCE.

"WE'VE BEEN MARCHING DAY AND NIGHT SINCE BRUSSELS. WHEN ARE WE GOING TO GET A REST?"

"DON'T MOAN! YOU'LL SLEEP BETTER AFTER A LONG WALK!"

BELGIUM WAS TAKEN. HOWEVER, THE STUBBORN RESISTANCE OF THE BELGIANS GAVE THE ALLIES, FRANCE AND BRITAIN, THE OPPORTUNITY TO TAKE COUNTER-MEASURES.

ON TO PARIS

While the Germans were overwhelming Belgium, the French marched into Alsace-Lorraine...

"THIS IS A HISTORIC MOMENT. WE'RE BACK ON THE BELOVED SOIL OF OUR LOST PROVINCES.*"

*THESE FRENCH TERRITORIES HAD BEEN LOST TO THE GERMANS IN 1871.

But on the 20th of August, six days after the French invasion, the Germans hit back!

Once again, the French had to abandon Alsace-Lorraine. Other French platoons engaged the Germans in combat in the Ardennes Forest. The French troops fought the German machine guns with naked bayonets!

"THEY GIVE US BAYONETS AGAINST THEIR MACHINE GUNS! IT'S PLAIN MURDER!"

The French were pushed back in the Ardennes. At the same time, the Germans destroyed the French military forces in the north.

"THEY SAY THAT ALL OUR ARMIES ARE ON THE RETREAT! AND YET WE THINK WE'RE SO INVINCIBLE!"

The French retreat went on for two weeks. The whole of northern France fell into German hands.

- Nothing can stop us now!
- On to Paris!

The military governor of Paris prepared the city for a siege. He advised the leaders of the government to leave.

- The Germans are getting nearer! You can hear their artillery from here. I cannot possibly guarantee your safety in the capital any longer!
- You're right. We're heading south straight away!

Whilst a great number of people abandoned the city, others stayed behind to man the barricades.

- You're mad! The Germans will be here in a couple of days!
- Then they will have to take our barricades first. They'll not get their hands on France's capital without a fight!

On the 4th of September, 1914, the French retreat came to an end. Marshal Joseph Joffre, the French commander-in-chief, called his generals to an evening meeting.

- The British are now at the front and we have reorganised our forces. Gentlemen... we shall make a stand along the Marne River.

THE ALLIED OFFENSIVE TOOK THE GERMANS BY SURPRISE.
HERR KOMMANDANT! THE FRENCH ARE ATTACKING!

AND THIS IS NOT JUST A LIGHTNING RAID! WE'RE BEING PUSHED BACK ALONG THE MARNE!
WE SHALL DIG OURSELVES IN ON THE NORTH BANK OF THE RIVER!

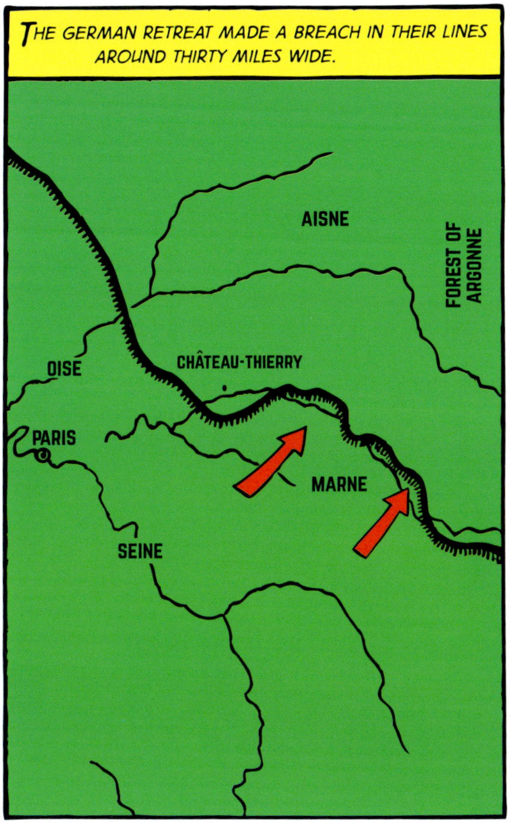
THE GERMAN RETREAT MADE A BREACH IN THEIR LINES AROUND THIRTY MILES WIDE.
AISNE
FOREST OF ARGONNE
OISE
CHÂTEAU-THIERRY
PARIS
MARNE
SEINE

THE ALLIES PUSHED THROUGH AND TRIED TO WIDEN THIS BREACH.

WE MUST KEEP ON FIGHTING, MY FRIEND! IF WE LOSE THIS BATTLE, FRANCE WILL FALL!

THE MAJORITY OF THE BRITISH FORCES HAD THEIR HANDS FULL. THE FRENCH HAD URGENT NEED OF REINFORCEMENTS TO SUPPORT THEIR BREAK-THROUGH.

FRENCH SOLDIERS ARE GIVING UP THEIR LIVES ALONG THE MARNE! SO WHY ARE THEY HOLDING US BACK HERE IN PARIS?

HOW CAN WE GET THERE? 60 KILOMETRES OF SOLID WALKING! WE ARE SHORT OF TRANSPORT!

AT MIDDAY ON THE 7TH OF SEPTEMBER, THE PARIS POLICE BEGAN TO REQUISITION SOME 600 TAXIS...

EXCUSE ME, SIR... FRANCE NEEDS YOUR TAXI!

EACH TAXI MADE TWO TRIPS TO THE MARNE, CARRYING FIVE SOLDIERS EACH TIME. AT NIGHT, AND OVER THE FOLLOWING WEEK, FRENCH REINFORCEMENTS REACHED THE BATTLEFIELDS.

SEE YOU LATER, DARLING! LOOK AFTER YOURSELF WHILE WE'RE BUSY WITH THE GERMANS!

WITH THEIR FRESH TROOPS, THE FRENCH MANAGED TO PUSH THE ENEMY BACK FROM THE MARNE.
DO WE HAVE TO LEAVE ALL OUR GUNS BEHIND?
IT LOOKS LIKE IT. I DON'T UNDERSTAND WHERE THE FRENCH HAVE FOUND ALL THESE SOLDIERS!
ON THE 7TH OF SEPTEMBER, THE GERMANS BEGAN AN ATTACK.
THEY WERE THROWN BACK BY A BARRAGE FROM THE FRENCH 75MM CANNONS.
THEY'RE RETREATING!
THE GERMANS FLED NORTH AND EAST. ALL TOWNS SOUTH OF THE MARNE WERE RECAPTURED BY THE FRENCH.
THIS IS THE TRUE HERO OF THIS BATTLE!

On the south-east extremity of the front, not far from the fortified town of Verdun, the Germans suffered heavy losses in an artillery bombardment.

On the evening of the 9th of September, the German troops marched on the attack again. But darkness and fog caused them to open fire on their own lines in confusion. The attack failed.

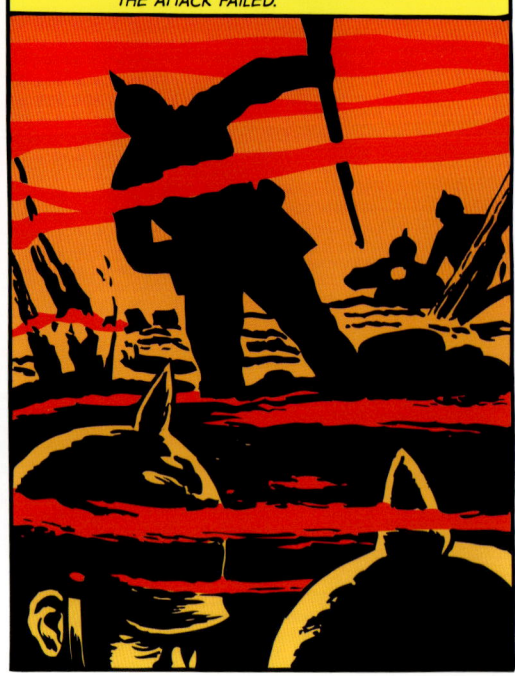

Three days later, the Germans reappeared on the north bank of the river Aisne. There, they dug themselves in and waited.

On the same day, the Allies reached the south bank of the river. They also dug themselves in.

THE BATTLE OF THE MARNE IS OVER! PARIS IS SAVED! LONG LIVE FRANCE!

ALL QUIET ON THE WESTERN FRONT

In the Great War, the fire power of machine guns and artillery made large movements of troops almost impossible. For four years, several million soldiers lived along the Western Front like moles in the ground. Scattered along the whole line, minor skirmishes continually flared up here and there...

In the most advanced trenches, men stood 24 hours a day within sight of the enemy on watch. The strip of ground between both lines was called No Man's Land, which was often no wider than 20 yards, sometimes hardly even ten.

"The lice will take care of you, if the Germans don't get you first!"

"Or you'll die of foot rot!"

At night, small patrols ventured out to capture part of a trench or take prisoners of war. The patrols had to clear a way through the deep shell-holes which had been gouged in No Man's Land, or work their way through thick barbed wire entanglements.

"If now and again you have to take cover in a shell-hole, make sure it's a dry one, or you might drown!"

But their position was often given away by "Very" lights. Then they made an easy target for enemy machine guns.

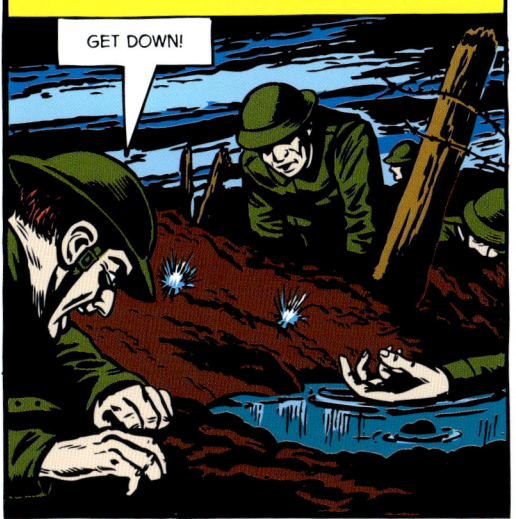

"Get down!"

If they were not called upon to serve in the trenches, the men remained in underground bunkers or caves.

"Apart from the mud, rats and exploding shells, it's quite homely here, isn't it?"

19

NOWHERE WAS SAFE ALONG THE WESTERN FRONT. EVERY DAY BROUGHT MORE VICTIMS OF SNIPERS OR ARTILLERY BOMBARDMENTS.

MORE AND MORE MEN ON BOTH SIDES WERE BROUGHT INTO THE TRENCHES. YOUNG GERMANS, FRENCH AND BRITISH GAVE UP THEIR LIVES FOR A FEW YARDS OF GROUND WHICH ONE HOUR LATER HAD TO BE ABANDONED AGAIN. MANY MEN WENT INSANE...

"WHY DON'T THEY ATTACK? WHERE ARE THEY HIDING?"

"THEY'RE PROBABLY WAITING UNTIL WE ATTACK. REAL FIGHTING HAS NO PART IN THIS WAR... WAIT AND DIE, THAT'S ALL IT IS!"

THERE WERE 7,000 DEAD OR WOUNDED IN THE TRENCHES EVERY DAY. EVERY DAY REPORTS FROM BOTH HEADQUARTERS STATED... "NO NEWS IN THE WEST... ALL QUIET ON THE WESTERN FRONT"!

THE RACE TO THE SEA

When the Germans discovered they couldn't reach Paris, they tried to capture the French ports along the English Channel. Without these ports Britain would no longer be able to bring supplies to her troops in France.

To begin with, the Belgian troops defended these ports. After the fall of Liège the Belgians had withdrawn to Antwerp which was also a fortified town. On the 28th of September, the Germans bombarded Antwerp.

The British sent a brigade of Marines to support the Belgians.

"That's the third German attack today! Why are we still here?"

"Because this is the last large town between the Germans and the sea. If they occupy the coast, our food supplies from Britain will grind to a halt!"

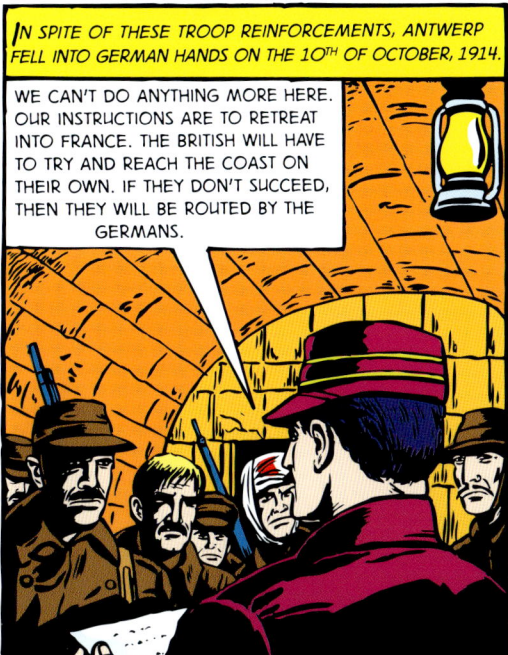

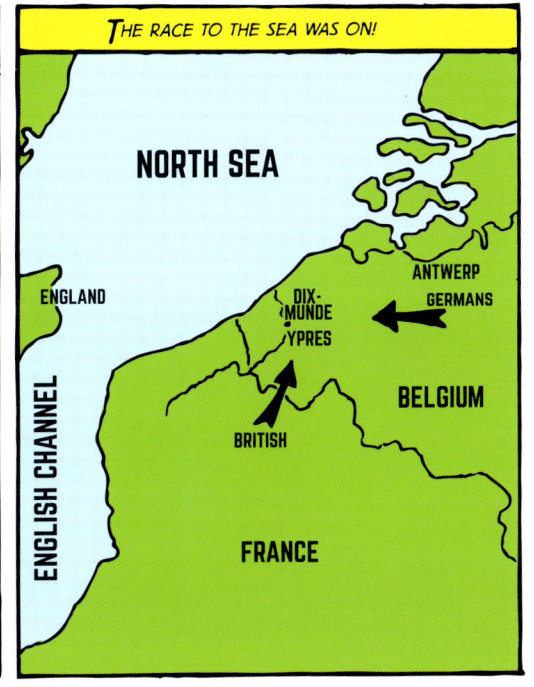

In spite of these troop reinforcements, Antwerp fell into German hands on the 10th of October, 1914.

"We can't do anything more here. Our instructions are to retreat into France. The British will have to try and reach the coast on their own. If they don't succeed, then they will be routed by the Germans."

The race to the sea was on!

NORTH SEA
ENGLAND
ENGLISH CHANNEL
DIXMUNDE
YPRES
ANTWERP
GERMANS
BRITISH
BELGIUM
FRANCE

The next German breakthrough came in Flanders, the flat region along the Belgian coast. On the 20th of October, the Germans made an attack on the Belgians and French who were defending Dixmunde on the river Yser. Waves of German troops surged forward, but the artillery mowed them all down.

"We'll have to pull back quick, but not before our cannons have claimed a few dozen victims!"

The Belgian front collapsed. The Germans advanced to the Yser.

In desperation, the British warship, HMS Venerable, moved right to the mouth of the river, where the German heavy artillery positions began their assault.

Under cover of the battle out to sea, the Belgians breached the dykes, which subsequently flooded the land. The Germans could get no further!

"If we can't hold back the Germans with our cannons, then we'll do it with seawater!"

22

Further south, the Germans reached Ypres. This town was an important junction for roads and canals which lay near the sea. However, the British had got there first!

On the 29th of October, the Germans tried to take possession of the hills around the town. They rained down shells on the British position.

At the same time, the Germans put in a mass attack on the hills. In the trenches stood troops from India, then a British colony, side by side with British soldiers. They waited until the Germans were near before opening fire.

"Keep calm! Wait for the order! Hold your guns ready!"

Suddenly the Germans ran into a hail of bullets. The British soldiers were well practised in firing off fifteen shots per minute. This barrage ripped huge holes in the German front lines.

"Fire!"

But the Germans kept coming over the bodies of the fallen, and took possession of the hill. General Douglas Haig, leader of the British troops, ordered a counter-attack. With bayonets fixed, the British stormed forward, beat off the attack and recaptured all lost ground.

During the night of the 30th of October, the Germans brought forward reinforcements made up of very young, patriotic recruits. They were all under the compulsory military age.

"I'd rather face death fighting for my country than have to live in a defeated Germany!"

The following morning, 300,000 men attacked the British positions on the hills. One wave after another of German soldiers was mown down, but there remained sufficient survivors to reach the British trenches and take them.

The British retreated into the woods in chaos. The Germans paused for breath and to regroup. The majority of the young recruits lay dead upon the hillside.

"We're fighting against children!"

At the beginning of November, the exhausted British troops were joined by French reinforcements. Among them were native soldiers from Morocco, which was then a French colony in North Africa.

THE GERMANS STILL HOPED FOR A QUICK VICTORY.

A NEW ORDER HAS JUST COME IN FROM HQ... FORCE A BREAK-THROUGH AT YPRES. CAPTURING THE CHANNEL PORTS WILL MEAN THE END OF THE WAR. GERMANY EXPECTS EACH MAN TO DO HIS DUTY.

IN THE GREY MORNING MIST OF THE 11TH OF NOVEMBER, THE GERMANS LAUNCHED ANOTHER HEAVY ARTILLERY AND INFANTRY ATTACK. BRITISH HIGH EXPLOSIVE SHELLS* AND HEAVY GUNFIRE POUNDED THE GERMAN ATTACKERS REPEATEDLY. HOWEVER, A DIVISION OF PRUSSIAN GUARDS MADE A BREACH IN THEIR LINES AND PUSHED THROUGH TO THE REARMOST TROOPS.

*SHELLS WHICH BURST AMONGST THE INFANTRY IN STEEL SPLINTERS.

EVERY AVAILABLE MAN RUSHED TO HELP CLOSE THE BREACH AGAIN. COOKS, POSTAL ORDERLIES, CLERKS AND OTHERS GATHERED FOR A COUNTER-ATTACK. THE BREACH WAS CLOSED AND THE DANGER PASSED.

A CAPTURED PRUSSIAN OFFICER ASKED OUT OF INTEREST WHAT THERE WAS BEYOND THE BRITISH CANNONS...

JUST A LITTLE SLICE OF BELGIUM!

IF ONLY WE HAD KNOWN!

On the 22nd of November, 1914, the German offensive was over. Before long, a strong line of trenches meandered over a distance of 600 miles from Switzerland to the North Sea.

At 12 o'clock on Christmas night, the men in the trenches began to sing. Beneath the awesome brilliance of the flares, the soldiers climbed out of their positions and went towards the enemy.

German and English soldiers met in No Man's Land and greeted each other heartily. They even played football!

MERRY CHRISTMAS!

THE SAME TO YOU, TOMMY!

Then they went back to their own trenches... and once again the shells screamed over their heads. This kind of shelling went on right to the end of the war.

The French channel ports were still in Allied hands. From the occupied Belgian ports, the Germans began to pose a very dangerous threat to the British supply routes.

THE SEA WOLVES

A FEW WEEKS AFTER GREAT BRITAIN HAD DECLARED WAR ON GERMANY, A GERMAN U-BOAT, OR SUBMARINE, MADE A TORPEDO ATTACK ON A CONVOY OF BRITISH SHIPS IN THE NORTH SEA. WITHIN HALF AN HOUR THREE BRITISH CRUISERS HAD BEEN SUNK.

IN OCTOBER 1914, GERMANY ORDERED HER U-BOATS TO PREVENT MERCHANT SHIPPING FROM GETTING SUPPLIES TO THE ALLIES. THE U-BOATS ADHERED TO THE RULES OF INTERNATIONAL CONVENTION. AS SOON AS THEY WERE ABOVE WATER, THEY FIRED A WARNING SHOT ACROSS THE BOWS OF THE MERCHANT SHIP.

"STOP ENGINES! PREPARE TO TAKE SURVIVORS ON BOARD!"

AT THAT POINT, THE U-BOAT GAVE THE CREW OF THE MERCHANT SHIP THE CHANCE TO ESCAPE.

"ARE YOU THINKING OF PUTTING YOUR OWN CREW ON BOARD?"

"WE HAVEN'T ENOUGH MEN FOR THAT. YOU'VE GOT 20 MINUTES TO ABANDON SHIP. WE'VE GOT TO SINK IT."

ONLY AFTER THIS DID THE U-BOAT OPEN FIRE BENEATH THE MERCHANT SHIP'S WATERLINE.

"THE SHIP IS SINKING. THAT'S ONE LESS CARGO FOR THE ALLIES!"

Britain was not in a fit state to provide all the food and raw materials needed to win a war. Without supplies from overseas she would never be able to keep going. In order to withstand the threat of the German U-boats, the British merchant ships were armed.

"The U-boat hasn't a cat in hell's chance. We've got heavier cannons!"

"The German commander should not have surfaced. He'd have done better to send us a torpedo!"

On the 17th of February, 1915, Germany declared the seas around Great Britain a war zone. She began by torpedoing all merchant shipping without prior warning, in flagrant violation of international law!

The Germans stationed the vast majority of their submarine fleet in the Baltic Sea. The remaining U-boats operated from harbours in Flanders, which the Allies had not been able to capture during the race for supremacy of the seas.

"The English coast is only 80 miles away. It won't be too difficult for us to attack their convoys on the Channel."

To protect their shipping routes from the U-boat menace, the British laid minefields and stretched out anti-submarine nets over the Straits of Dover, the narrowest section of the English Channel.

The Straits of Dover were soon free of U-boats, but the problem of Allied supplies was not completely solved. At that time the need for supplies also began along the Eastern Front.

28

THE EASTERN FRONT

Russia started the war with more men but fewer resources than any of the other countries. Her mobilisation and all other preparations for war took place very slowly, since there were no modern railways or heavy industries. Although Russia had only 2 million of her 20 million soldiers armed, she attacked Germany in August 1914.

The Russians marched out of Poland, then still a Russian province, into Germany's most easterly zone, known as East Prussia.

"My men have no shoes on their feet! Why are they sending us to fight so unprepared?"

"For now, the French want us to shoot some Germans on their behalf. That's what they've told the Tsar* and the message has got through to us. That's all I know."

*THE RUSSIAN EMPEROR

The Russian hordes pushed immediately into East Prussia from the north, and wiped out the small German garrison at Gumbinnen.

On the 20th of August, the very same day, a second Russian force under the command of General A. V. Samsonov attacked from the south.

The German commander in East Prussia requested reinforcements from the west.

"As quickly as possible! If the two Russian armies merge, we'll be surrounded!"

PAUL VON HINDENBURG, A FORMER GERMAN GENERAL, WITHDREW FROM HIS SQUAD TO TAKE UP COMMAND ON THE EASTERN FRONT... GENERAL LUDENDORFF, WHO HAD CAPTURED LIÈGE, BECAME HINDENBURG'S RIGHT-HAND MAN.
THE RUSSIAN ARMY IN THE NORTH HAS NOT ADVANCED SINCE OVERRUNNING GUMBINNEN.
WHY SHOULDN'T WE TAKE THE RISK? LET'S JUST LEAVE A DETACHMENT OF CAVALRY BEHIND TO DISTRACT THE RUSSIAN TROOPS IN THE NORTH AND THE REST OF OUR FORCES CAN WIPE OUT SAMSONOV IN THE SOUTH.

JUST AS THE GERMANS HAD HOPED, SAMSONOV LED HIS ARMY INTO THE WOODLANDS NEAR THE GERMAN TOWN OF TANNENBERG. ON THE 26TH OF AUGUST, RUSSIAN PATROLS PUSHED FORWARD TOWARDS VON HINDENBURG'S ARMY.
I HAVE HERE A TELEGRAM FROM GENERAL SAMSONOV. HE SAYS THERE ARE ONLY A FEW GERMANS IN THE WOODS. ALL UNITS MUST START AN ATTACK!

HOWEVER, SAMSONOV HAD NOT THOUGHT TO PUT HIS TELEGRAM INTO CODE, SO IT WAS INTERCEPTED BY THE GERMANS.
TAKE THIS IMMEDIATELY TO GENERAL HINDENBURG'S HEADQUARTERS. IT'S THE PLANS AND POSITIONS OF GENERAL SAMSONOV!

THE FOLLOWING DAY, THE RUSSIANS REALISED THAT THEY HAD FALLEN INTO A TRAP IN THE WOODS OF TANNENBERG.

THE BATTLE WAS SOON OVER. THE GERMANS TOOK 90,000 PRISONERS OF WAR AND 100 CANNONS. SAMSONOV'S ARMY WAS COMPLETELY ANNIHILATED.

BUT SAMSONOV HIMSELF WAS NOT AMONG THEM...

THERE IS NO OTHER SOLUTION! I CAN NO LONGER LOOK THE TSAR IN THE FACE AFTER THE LOSS OF ALL MY FORCES!

HINDENBURG NEEDED MORE TROOPS IF HE WAS TO DRIVE THE RUSSIANS OUT OF NORTHERN PRUSSIA. HE GOT TWO ARMY CORPS AND A UNIT OF CAVALRY FROM THE WESTERN FRONT AS SUPPORT.

THIS IS A GOOD DEAL EASIER THAN ON THE FRONT ALONG THE MARNE!

BETWEEN THE 6TH AND 15TH OF SEPTEMBER, WHILE THE GERMAN ARMIES IN THE WEST WERE ON THE RETREAT ALONG THE MARNE, THE GERMAN ARMY IN THE EAST DEFEATED THE RUSSIANS IN THE BATTLE OF THE MASURIAN LAKES. PRUSSIA WAS FREE OF ENEMY SOLDIERS.

ALTHOUGH THE RUSSIANS DID NOT MANAGE TO OCCUPY PRUSSIA, THEIR ATTACK SUPPORTED THE ALLIED WAR EFFORT IN THE WEST. GERMAN TROOPS, URGENTLY NEEDED ON THE MARNE, WERE NOW DYING ON THE EASTERN FRONT.

BACK TO THE BALKANS

The Russians had more success against the Austrians. On the 1st of September, 1914, Russian units attacked the town of Lemberg, in the Austrian province of Galicia.

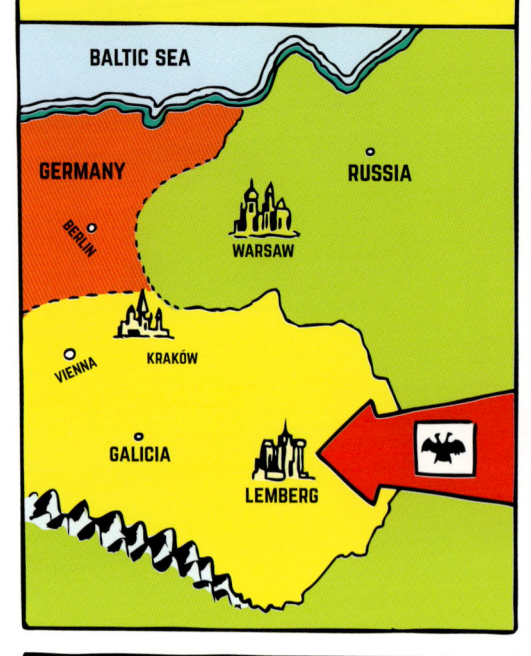

The battle between the Russians and Austrians around Lemberg lasted two days.

The town fell on the 3rd of September, and the Russians made a triumphant entry. The name of the town was changed to Lvov.

Now the town's got a Slavic name again!

That'll soon be the case with all towns in Galicia! We must free the Slavic people!

The victorious Russian armies pushed on through Galicia towards the west. On the 6th of September, the Russians came face-to-face with two Austrian armies which were retreating from Poland. The Austrians were completely routed!

I thought we were just up against the Serbs.

I thought so too. But we should have expected this!

There were Serbs in the Austrian army who refused to fight against the Russians!

"PICK UP YOUR GUN OR I'LL SEE YOU HANGED FOR TREASON!"

"I'D RATHER HANG AS A TRAITOR THAN SHOOT A SLAV! THAT WOULD BE TREACHERY!"

The Austrian army, undermined by mutiny and breaches of discipline amongst its leaders, remained on the retreat.

"THE RUSSIANS ARE PLANNING TO PUSH ON TO KRAKÓW. WE'LL GO BACK 80 MILES TO THE WEST AND TRY TO DEFEND KRAKÓW!"

"YES, THE CITY IS THE KEY TO BERLIN AND VIENNA. IT MUST NOT FALL INTO RUSSIAN HANDS."

The Russians followed on foot. During September, they conquered the last two fortresses in Galicia.

Towards the end of the month, virtually the whole of Galicia was in their hands. Their troops prepared to storm Kraków and also the prosperous German province of Silesia on the other side of the Austrian border.

However, the Germans had no intention of putting a high price on Silesia. At the beginning of October, Hindenburg and Ludendorff were instructed to save Austria from defeat and bring the Russian offensive to a halt. More troops came from the west to form a new German army.

An attack of our own is the only way to stop the Russian steam-roller. We shall invade Poland.

Again Russian carelessness played into German hands. Secret documents were found on the body of a dead Russian officer. These revealed the positions and instructions of all Russian units.

Even a whole army of spies could not assemble so much information!

On the 15th of October, Hindenburg went on the attack over a wide front, from north to south, diagonally across the extreme west of Poland. Their target was Warsaw, the capital.

For three days, the fighting alternated over each front. The weather conditions were terrible. Roads were impassable with mud. The Russians halted the Germans by the Vistula River, about 6 miles away from Warsaw.

On the 20th of October, Hindenburg gave his troops the order to retreat to the German border in Silesia. On their way back, the Germans destroyed roads and railway lines, so that the Russians could not pursue them.

Hindenburg had hoped he could give the Kaiser Warsaw as a Christmas present. On the 11th of November, with reinforcements sent to him from the west, he attacked again. But on this occasion the Russians held firm 6 miles to the west of Warsaw.

The fierce cold of the Polish winter put an end to warmongering.

We have not taken Warsaw but we have stopped the Russian advance. Silesia is safe and we've conquered a large slice of Poland. Next year everything will be ours and we'll drive the Russians out of Galicia.

The fighting ability of the Russians was greater than expected. However, by the end of 1914 they had run out of war materiel. Only one Russian in ten had a weapon. Supplies were essential!

So far, we've had to send off supplies without bread and footwear, but fighting without weapons is not on!

The Allies began to send supplies to the Russians at top speed...

This'll help you tie down quite a few Germans on the Eastern Front!

Yes, but now that the Germans have blockaded our supply ports in the north, we've only got the Black Sea route left. If anything goes wrong with that, Russia is doomed!

SHIPS VERSUS FORTS

In October 1914, Turkey joined the war on the side of the Germans. The Turks blockaded the Russian ports on the Black Sea, which the Allies could no longer use to supply the Russians.

In January 1915, the British drew up a plan for an attack on the Dardanelles, the narrow straits between the Mediterranean and the Black Sea.

"Since we can't withdraw any troops from the Western Front, the British Navy will have to carry out the attack on this occasion."

"If we manage to destroy the Turkish forts on both sides of the Dardanelles, we'll be able to force a break-through to the Russian ports."

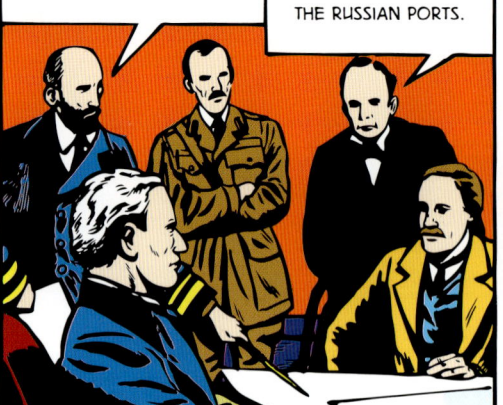

At the start of February, a fleet of fifteen British and four French warships met in the Mediterranean. Among them was the Queen Elizabeth, a great armoured battleship which had the heaviest cannons in the British Navy. It belonged to a type known as super iron-clads.

"Poor Turks! I wouldn't like to be caught in the crossfire of these cannons!"

On the 19th of February, the fleet steamed towards the Dardanelles. The heavy battleships began a bombardment of the Turkish forts guarding the entrance. The forts returned their fire.

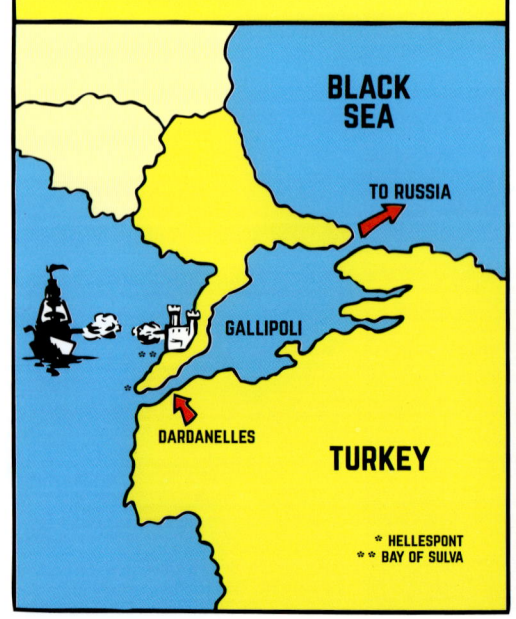

BLACK SEA
TO RUSSIA
GALLIPOLI
DARDANELLES
TURKEY
* HELLESPONT
** BAY OF SULVA

One week later, the forts had been silenced. A squad of British soldiers landed on the north side of the straits. They found the forts abandoned and blew them apart with their cannons.

36

A FEW DAYS LATER, THE QUEEN ELIZABETH OPENED LONG-DISTANCE FIRE ON A SECOND LINE OF FORTS WHICH LAY ALONG THE NARROW STRAITS WHERE THE DARDANELLES WERE ONLY A FEW KILOMETRES IN WIDTH.

SAILING THROUGH THESE NARROW STRAITS IS THE MOST DANGEROUS JOB OF ALL. THE TURKS HAVE MOUNTED THEIR HEAVIEST CANNONS HERE. ONCE WE'RE PAST HERE, WE'LL BE SAFE!

THE NARROW PASSAGEWAY WAS BLOCKED BY TURKISH MINEFIELDS. BRITISH TRAWLERS WERE COMMANDEERED TO CLEAR THE MINES AND THUS OPEN UP A PATH FOR THE WARSHIPS.

ON THE MORNING OF THE 18TH OF MARCH, THE WHOLE FLEET TRAVELLED THROUGH THE DARDANELLES TO THE NARROW STRAITS. FOR SEVERAL HOURS, THE SHIPS BOMBARDED THE FORTS ALONG THE COAST FROM SHORT RANGE. AT FIRST, THE FORTS WERE STILL FIGHTING BACK, BUT AT MIDDAY THE TURKISH CANNONS FELL SILENT.

SIGNAL TO THE FLEET THAT WE CAN STEAM THROUGH.

BUT THEN FATE STRUCK. THE FORTS BEGAN FIRING AGAIN...

The Turks re-opened fire. Three heavy shells and a floating mine signalled the end for the French battleship Bouvet. The ship sank inside two minutes.

Soon after, the British warships Irresistible and Ocean strayed into a minefield. Both ships capsized and sank.

Meanwhile, the Turkish coastal batteries set the battleship Inflexible on fire, and made a gaping hole in the French ship, Gaulois, just above the waterline. Several other ships were to suffer direct hits before they saw the opportunity to turn round in the narrow straits and escape.

At sunset on the 18th of March, the remaining ships of the combined Anglo-French battle fleet beat a retreat through the Dardanelles Straits, out of reach of the Turkish batteries.

Driven by necessity, Britain sent troops to the Dardanelles region. She was hoping that a land campaign would succeed where the naval forces had failed.

Have you any idea where we're going?

Gallipoli, I think. It must be somewhere on the coast...

THE TURKISH TRAGEDY

While the British were preparing for the invasion, the Turks were also getting ready. This was happening under the watchful eye of a German general.

THE BRITISH OBJECTIVE WILL PROBABLY BE THE FORT ON THE WESTERN SIDE OF THE STRAITS. WE SHALL ESTABLISH A PROTECTIVE BELT OF CAMOUFLAGED TRENCHES AND GUN EMPLACEMENTS.

In the early morning of the 25th of April, 1915, the first landing party, an ANZAC company, set foot on the beach.*

THIS IS NOT THE RIGHT PLACE. WE'RE A MILE AWAY FROM THE TARGET. WHOSE FAULT IS IT?

I DON'T KNOW. THERE ISN'T MUCH WE CAN DO REALLY. WE MIGHT AS WELL CLIMB THOSE CLIFFS.

*AUSTRALIAN AND NEW ZEALAND ARMY CORPS

On the same day, the British landed at the Hellespont 15 miles south. As soon as the boats reached the shore, the Turks opened fire.

PUSH AHEAD TO THE BEACH! WE'RE IN THE MIDDLE OF BARBED WIRE, SO STAY IN THE BOATS!

The British managed to form a bridgehead. They were later joined by the French, but didn't manage to make any headway against the entrenched Turks.

IN THREE WEEKS WE HAVEN'T EVEN ADVANCED 300 YARDS! THIS IS FAR WORSE THAN ON THE MARNE!

I THINK TURKEY HAS MADE AN ALLIANCE WITH THE FLIES HERE. THEY'RE AT LEAST AS BAD AS THE BULLETS!

THE BRITISH WERE SHORT OF ARTILLERY AND DEPENDENT UPON THE CANNONS ON BOARD THE WARSHIPS WHICH LAY AT ANCHOR OUTSIDE THE LANDING ZONES. HOWEVER, IN MAY, A GERMAN U-BOAT CAME ALL THE WAY FROM ITS BASE IN THE NORTH SEA AND SANK TWO BRITISH WARSHIPS.

AND WE THOUGHT WE WERE SAFE AND SOUND HERE FROM GERMAN SUBMARINE ATTACKS!

EVERY INFANTRY MOVEMENT NOW BECAME FUTILE. DURING THE FIRST WEEK OF JUNE, THE FINAL BRITISH OFFENSIVE RAN AGROUND IN THE FACE OF THE TURKISH CANNONS.

THE ALLIED TROOPS SUFFERED BADLY FROM THE SWARMS OF FLIES, THE HEAT AND THE SHORTAGE OF FOOD AND WATER. THE HOSPITALS WERE FULL TO OVERFLOWING.

DO YOU KNOW, SIR, THAT AT THIS MOMENT WE ARE LOSING TWICE AS MANY MEN TO ALL SORTS OF ILLNESSES AS WE ARE TO BATTLE CASUALTIES?

THE BRITISH DECIDED TO ABANDON THE TWO BRIDGEHEADS THEY HAD UNSUCCESSFULLY BUILT, AND LANDED A NEW REGIMENT FURTHER TO THE NORTH. ON THE 6TH OF AUGUST, THE ALLIES WENT ASHORE AT THE BAY OF SULVA.

Neither the soldiers nor their officers had any experience of war. No-one knew exactly what his task was. Some men went sunbathing on the beach, whilst the officers simply brewed tea.

"What are the orders for today?"

"I wish I knew. I've had none at all! We might as well all go swimming!"

Although battles were frequently fought in the summer, the Allies achieved not one of their intended objectives. With the autumn came the rainy season and all activity ground to a halt. The British War Minister, the Earl Kitchener, arrived in person at the elevated positions in Gallipoli.

"Our troops are occupying only the edge of the coastal strip. The Turks are in total control of the territory. Instruct the men to make a complete withdrawal!"

But before the British had the opportunity to withdraw, fate struck again. At the end of November Gallipoli was hit by a blizzard.

"Hurry up, Sergeant! Where are the rest of your men?"

"Dead, sir! All drowned in their trenches!"

In the five weeks that followed, the remaining troops marched away from Gallipoli, leaving behind 200,000 dead along the rocky coastline. The Gallipoli disaster meant that Russia would not receive the supply of weapons which she needed so badly. The war along the Eastern Front would not produce victory.

SECRET WEAPONS

The war had also fallen into a rut in the west. In 1915, neither side gained any territory. Hundreds of thousands of men fell on both sides. New weapons were tested to help get the war going again along the western front.

The new German weapon was poison gas. On the evening of the 22nd of April, 1915, a green mist drifted low over the ground in the direction of the French and Canadian troops on the front near Ypres. This was deadly mustard gas, released from cylindrical containers positioned behind the German lines. Unprotected soldiers scrambled out of the trenches along a 4-mile width of the front. Gasping for breath, they fell dead. From that day on, both sides used all sorts of poison gas and gas masks formed part of the standard equipment of everyone in the trenches.

In 1915, the British began to build a number of remarkable vehicles. In order to mislead the German spies, they let it be known that they were busy constructing a new sort of fuel tank. The name "tank" stuck! In fact, tanks were mobile machine gun posts. Under enemy fire, they were able to break through barbed-wire entanglements and ride over trenches. On the 15th of September, 1916, the first tanks were thrown forward into battle. They frightened and dismayed the Germans, but they were too slow to be effective. Nevertheless, the British were convinced that this tank was a way of putting an end to the stalemate in the war of the trenches.

THEY SHALL NOT PASS

IN 1916, THE ALLIES HAD SUFFICIENT RESERVES FOR A NEW OFFENSIVE ON THE WESTERN FRONT. AT THAT TIME, THE GERMANS HAD THRUST BACK THE RUSSIANS AND THEY WERE ABLE TO TRANSPORT A MILLION SOLDIERS FROM THE EASTERN FRONT TO THE WEST. THEY FIRST WENT ON THE ATTACK OVER BY VERDUN.

VERDUN, ON THE RIVER MEUSE, WAS THE BIGGEST FORTIFIED FRENCH TOWN ON THE GERMAN BORDER. NEARBY, ON THE HILLS, LAY A DOUBLE RING OF DEFENSIVE POSITIONS. ON THE NORTHERN SIDE OF THESE POSITIONS, THE FRENCH DUG EXTENSIVE TRENCHES.

THERE WAS A SPECIAL REASON WHY VERDUN WAS CHOSEN AS A FOCUS OF ATTACK BY THE GERMANS...

"WE MUST BLEED THE FRENCH TO DEATH. SO, WE MUST CHOOSE A PLACE WHICH IS SO IMPORTANT TO THEM THAT THEY WILL BE READY TO DEFEND IT TO THE LAST MAN. THAT PLACE IS VERDUN!"

THE ATTACK TOOK THE FRENCH BY SURPRISE. ON THE 21ST OF FEBRUARY, THE FRENCH LINE ON THE RIGHT BANK OF THE MEUSE SUDDENLY CAME UNDER HEAVY ARTILLERY FIRE OVER ITS 15-MILE LENGTH.

A FEW HOURS LATER, GERMAN PATROLS CROSSED OVER NO MAN'S LAND TO FIND OUT THE SITUATION IN THE FRENCH TRENCHES.

"THE FURTHEST FORWARD ENEMY LINE IS COMPLETELY DESTROYED. OUR TROOPS CAN NOW ADVANCE."

On the 25th of February, the Germans conquered Fort Douaumont, a key position in the outermost defensive cordon.

The loss of this fort caused great turmoil among the French. On the evening of its surrender, a new general, Henri Pétain, was put in charge of the defence of Verdun.

Reinforcement of our troops is our only means of salvation! Our motto must be: "THEY SHALL NOT PASS"!

The following day, the French undertook a counter-attack and they swept the Germans off Douaumont Hill. For four days the Germans tried to win back the ground, but were kept at bay by the artillery.

Call a halt to the attack on Douaumont! The French guns are claiming too many lives!

The French were ready to fight for every yard of ground, but during the battle their supplies ran out. The Germans cut off the railway links, so thousands of volunteers maintained the flow of supplies via any surviving route.

That's the way to Verdun now, my boy. We're calling it the Sacred Road.

On the west bank of the Meuse, three hills separated the Germans from the town of Verdun. On the 6th of March, the Germans made an attack on the so-called "Hill of Death", the most important of the three. However, this time the element of surprise was lacking, so the French artillery was able to engage the enemy in battle. The bitter struggle lasted all week and in the end the Germans failed to take the hill.

On the east bank of the river, the Germans pushed in a southerly direction to Fort Vaux, which formed part of the outer defensive ring. There they came to a standstill. Both sides were close to exhaustion.

The French had a stroke of luck around this time when a German ammunition dump was blown up. 450,000 heavy shells exploded without even one French soldier losing his life.

In the middle of April, the Germans prepared a new offensive on the hills west of Verdun. On the 18th of April, after heavy artillery bombardment, twelve German infantry regiments started an attack. French machine gun fire from the hard-pressed trenches thrust the Germans back. By the end of April, the Germans had advanced by no more than half a mile west of the Meuse.

The fort situated inside Verdun was a place where the French soldiers could rest. This was one advantage the French had over the Germans. Throughout the battle, the men could at least eat and sleep safe in the rooms deep inside the fort.

"Welcome to the Grand Hotel!"

"Just wait till the Germans over there show you a sample of their hospitality!"

In May, the Germans attacked on both sides of the Meuse. For 12 hours the French lines lay under the murderous fire of 60 German batteries.

"We shall capture Verdun, even if we have to use all our cannons and shells!"

Five new German infantry divisions stormed the Hill of Death and conquered the summit. However, the French carried on fighting along the southern slopes.

To the west of the Meuse, the Germans released the French grip on the fort at Douaumont. On the 7th of June, Fort Vaux fell. The Germans had now captured two positions on the outer defensive ring.

"We wouldn't have surrendered if we hadn't been short of water!"

46

The next German attack was directed on Fort Souville in the inner defensive ring. On the 20th of June, the Germans used deadly phosgene gas against the French artillery guarding the fort. Thousands of Frenchmen fell victim to it... and their cannons were silenced.

On the 23rd of June, the Germans occupied Fleury, a little town in the immediate vicinity of Fort Souville. Both the fort and Verdun were at risk.

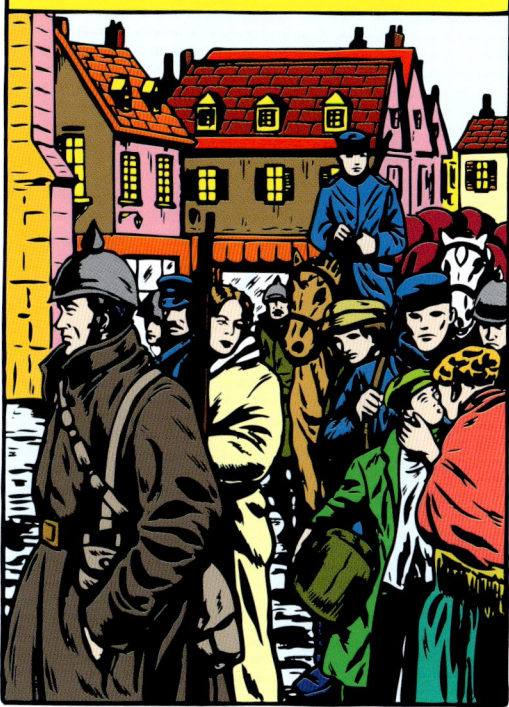

General Pétain appealed to General Haig, the new British commander in France.

"Any further German advance could mean the fall of Verdun and a threat to the Allied front. We'll have to tie the Germans down in another sector!"

On the 24th of June, the British cannons began a bombardment along the river Somme, nearly 120 miles north-west. The supply of German reinforcements to Verdun stopped, and the attacks also became weaker.

But the battle was not over yet... General Robert Nivelle took over command of the French forces at Verdun. On the 17th of August, he drove the Germans out of Fleury.

Then, on the 25th of October, the French recaptured the fort at Douaumont and, on the 2nd of November, Fort Vaux.

"THE GERMANS NEEDED FOUR MONTHS TO CONQUER THIS TERRITORY AND WE'VE WON IT BACK IN A COUPLE OF DAYS!"

The Battle of Verdun ended in December 1916. More than 400,000 French troops were killed or wounded, but the Germans did not pass!

However, the worst slaughter in this great war had only just begun! Thousands would lose their lives with no other purpose than to kill as many of the enemy as possible. Military objectives were forgotten... the one who could hold out longest... would win!

48

THE BATTLE OF THE SOMME

In 1916, the British decided to force the Germans into a war of attrition, just as the Germans had done to the French at Verdun.

General Pétain has asked if we can start two days earlier than was originally agreed. Our bombardment will now begin on the 24th of June.

Along a front 15 miles wide, the German positions came under British barrage. This was along the River Somme. The British bombardment lasted seven days, but a significant number of shells did not explode.

That's the tenth dud shell today!

The British infantry will find it odd when they see we're still alive!

At half past seven on the morning of the 1st of July, 60,000 British soldiers climbed out of their trenches and ran towards the German lines.

As they approached, the Germans sprang to life in their trenches. Incessant fire from machine guns and cannons carved great holes in the British ranks. In one day, the British lost 60,000 men! This battle lasted throughout the summer. The British gained only 6 miles at the cost of 675,000 men.

However, the British military leaders deemed the operation a success... the Germans had lost 700,000 men!

DAY OF THE IRONCLADS

Both sides now strove to exhaust each other just as in the battles of Verdun and the Somme, and command of the sea gained more and more importance.

Britain and Germany were the two mightiest seafaring nations of the world. At the start of the war the British Home Fleet completely paralysed the German navy.

The German admirals tried everything to destroy the British Home Fleet.

If we could just break the blockade, we would also be able to prevent supplies from Britain. But sadly their fleet is too strong!

We ought to be able to destroy the ships one by one. The best thing would be to send a flotilla of cruisers to the Danish coast. The British will order their cruisers to meet them. Then our ironclads will emerge and sink the British.

In the early morning of the 31st of May, 1916, the two enemy flotillas steamed into the North Sea for their encounter. At 2:20pm Admiral David Beatty received an urgent message on his flagship...

The enemy has been sighted off the Danish coast, sir, heading east-south-east.

Send a seaplane off to take the exact number and location of the ships.

A seaplane was lowered onto the waves from one of the other ships, and a little later it rose into the air.

THE SEAPLANE FIXED THE PRECISE LOCATION OF THE FLOTILLA OF GERMAN CRUISERS.

SIR, THE SEAPLANE HAS JUST SIGNALLED THAT FIVE ENEMY BATTLE-CRUISERS HAVE BEEN SPOTTED WITH AN ESCORT OF TORPEDO BOATS!

CHANGE COURSE. WE'RE GOING AFTER THEM!

THE TWO SQUADRONS MET OFF THE COAST OF THE JUTLAND PENINSULA. BOTH SIDES OPENED FIRE SIMULTANEOUSLY!

WITHIN A FEW MINUTES TWO BRITISH BATTLECRUISERS HAD BEEN HIT. THEY EXPLODED AND SANK AT ONCE.

MEANWHILE THE MAIN BODY OF THE GERMAN BATTLE FLEET STEAMED NORTH TO JOIN IN THE CONFLICT.

OUR PLAN'S WORKING. THE BRITISH HAVE FALLEN INTO THE TRAP!

The main German force arrived at the scene of the battle at 4pm.

The Germans are trying to lure us into a trap, but we shall turn the tables on them! We'll set our course towards the north and join up with Admiral Jellicoe's home fleet.

Admiral John Jellicoe, First Sea Lord of the British Grand Fleet, hurried to help Beatty's flotilla of cruisers. By 6:30pm in the evening, the two British fleets had come together.

We've now got the Germans surrounded! Give the order to attack!

The battle raged on despite increasing darkness. Nearly 250 ships took part. The British endeavoured to manoeuvre themselves between the German fleet and its home bases. The German ships tried to break free.

The German ships were fewer in number. Admiral Reinhard von Scheer, commander of the German Atlantic Fleet, decided on a last desperate effort.

Attention! All destroyers must aim their weapons at the British. The cruisers must take up a position between Jellicoe and our ironclads. It's do or die! Our Atlantic fleet must be saved!

At about 9pm, Von Scheer turned about and attacked the weakest sector of Jellicoe's fleet. The German ironclads cleared a way through the escort of British destroyers.

Suddenly five German ships appeared to starboard of the British cruiser Southampton.

They trained their searchlights on their quarry and opened fire from a short distance.

The Southampton's gun-turrets had to take a great number of direct hits, which took the lives of many gunners.

One shell landed right by the bridge, and fire broke out. The flames reached high up to the crow's nest.

I'VE SEEN THREE SHIPS BLOWN UP TODAY, AND I WONDER IF WE'RE GOING TO BE THE FOURTH!

QUITE LIKELY! IT'S SO HOT HERE ON THE BRIDGE THAT MY FEET ARE ALL COVERED IN BLISTERS!

Just as suddenly as it had begun, the attack ended. The searchlights were extinguished, and the enemy ships disappeared. The whole operation had only lasted five minutes, but the Southampton had had to take ten direct hits. 52 crew were killed and 85 wounded.

The whole night long ships on both sides were sunk by shells or torpedoes. In the darkness, the German fleet saw its opportunity to escape.

By daybreak the British fleet lay isolated upon the lonely sea...

SEND THE FOLLOWING MESSAGE TO THE ADMIRALTY... "THE ENEMY FLEET HAS ESCAPED. WE'RE HEADING FOR PORT."

The Germans lost 11 ships and the British 14 in the Battle of Jutland. Both sides claimed victory. However, the German Atlantic fleet did not venture out again during the rest of the war!

54

THE ATLANTIC SUPPLY ROUTE

After the U-boats had been driven out of the Straits of Dover, they began to attack shipping off the southern coast of Ireland, on the supply routes to Great Britain.

On the 7th of May, 1915, the German submarines were to be found in these very waters. At 2:30 in the afternoon the commander spotted an ocean liner.

*There's a large passenger ship in neutral waters. I can clearly see its four funnels. We have been instructed to sink any ship that crosses our path. Number one torpedo... **FIRE!***

The ship was shaken into confusion by two violent explosions when the torpedo smashed a hole in the boilers. It was the Lusitania, an unarmed British passenger ship, which was carrying 1,900 passengers and crew from New York to Liverpool. Half the passengers were women and children...

Less than 20 minutes after the torpedo struck, the Lusitania disappeared beneath the waves. Nearly 1,200 people lost their lives.

The result of this tragic loss was that several neutral countries turned against Germany. This was particularly the case with the United States, because among the dead of the Lusitania were 128 Americans.

The Germans are mass murderers! America must declare war on Germany at once after this awful incident!

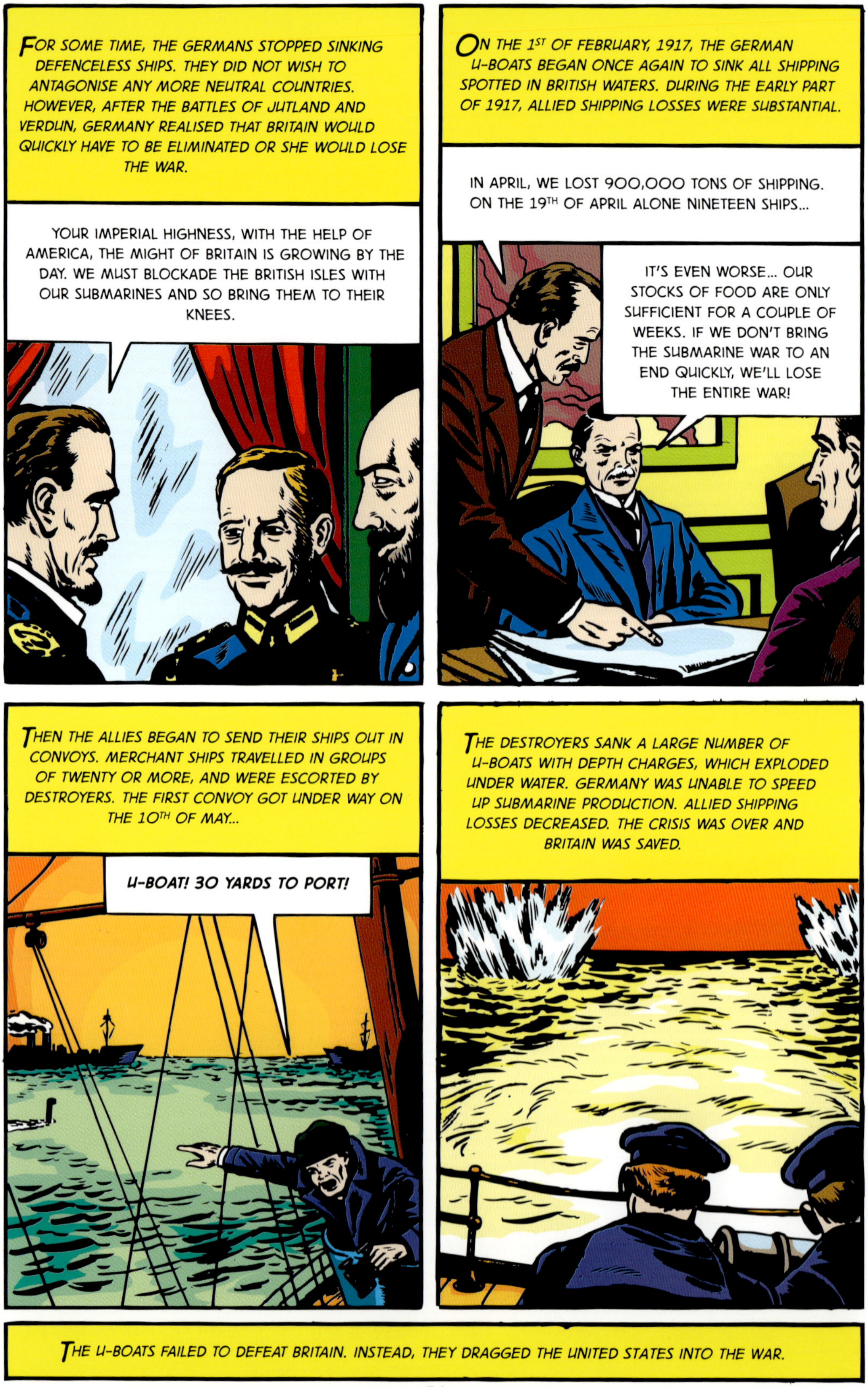
FOR SOME TIME, THE GERMANS STOPPED SINKING DEFENCELESS SHIPS. THEY DID NOT WISH TO ANTAGONISE ANY MORE NEUTRAL COUNTRIES. HOWEVER, AFTER THE BATTLES OF JUTLAND AND VERDUN, GERMANY REALISED THAT BRITAIN WOULD QUICKLY HAVE TO BE ELIMINATED OR SHE WOULD LOSE THE WAR.
YOUR IMPERIAL HIGHNESS, WITH THE HELP OF AMERICA, THE MIGHT OF BRITAIN IS GROWING BY THE DAY. WE MUST BLOCKADE THE BRITISH ISLES WITH OUR SUBMARINES AND SO BRING THEM TO THEIR KNEES.
ON THE 1ST OF FEBRUARY, 1917, THE GERMAN U-BOATS BEGAN ONCE AGAIN TO SINK ALL SHIPPING SPOTTED IN BRITISH WATERS. DURING THE EARLY PART OF 1917, ALLIED SHIPPING LOSSES WERE SUBSTANTIAL.
IN APRIL, WE LOST 900,000 TONS OF SHIPPING. ON THE 19TH OF APRIL ALONE NINETEEN SHIPS...
IT'S EVEN WORSE... OUR STOCKS OF FOOD ARE ONLY SUFFICIENT FOR A COUPLE OF WEEKS. IF WE DON'T BRING THE SUBMARINE WAR TO AN END QUICKLY, WE'LL LOSE THE ENTIRE WAR!
THEN THE ALLIES BEGAN TO SEND THEIR SHIPS OUT IN CONVOYS. MERCHANT SHIPS TRAVELLED IN GROUPS OF TWENTY OR MORE, AND WERE ESCORTED BY DESTROYERS. THE FIRST CONVOY GOT UNDER WAY ON THE 10TH OF MAY...
U-BOAT! 30 YARDS TO PORT!
THE DESTROYERS SANK A LARGE NUMBER OF U-BOATS WITH DEPTH CHARGES, WHICH EXPLODED UNDER WATER. GERMANY WAS UNABLE TO SPEED UP SUBMARINE PRODUCTION. ALLIED SHIPPING LOSSES DECREASED. THE CRISIS WAS OVER AND BRITAIN WAS SAVED.
THE U-BOATS FAILED TO DEFEAT BRITAIN. INSTEAD, THEY DRAGGED THE UNITED STATES INTO THE WAR.

THE YANKS ARE COMING

Most people in the United States saw the war as a European matter which didn't concern them. They agreed with the declaration of neutrality made by President Wilson in 1914.

"We didn't want this war and we don't represent a threat to anyone either. We have no territorial ambitions and we must remain neutral!"

But as the war dragged on, the American public took sides. There were some who stood behind Germany.

"Great Britain is waging war in order to uphold her colonial power. She is obstructing American voyages to Germany. The British are nothing but pirates!"

However, other Americans supported the Allied cause.

"The Germans are brutal destroyers of civilisation. We must choose to side with democratic countries like Britain and France!"

The torpedoing of the Lusitania brought the United States closer to the Allies. President Wilson sent Germany a memo in which he demanded that the German U-boats should only attack warships. Some Americans reacted even more vehemently to the sinking of the Lusitania.

In 1917, the Germans resumed their ruthless submarine war. In March of that year, the German U-boats sank five American merchant ships. The majority of Americans were now well and truly convinced that the United States should side with the Allies.

"World democracy must be safeguarded. We shall enter the war to put an end to it once and for all!"

On the 6th of April, 1917, the United States declared war on the German Empire!

IN APRIL 1917, THERE WERE ONLY 92,000 MEN SERVING IN THE AMERICAN ARMY.

IN MAY, THE AMERICAN CONGRESS PASSED A LAW MAKING MILITARY CONSCRIPTION COMPULSORY FOR ALL MALE NATIONALS BETWEEN THE AGES OF 21 AND 31. MORE THAN NINE AND A HALF MILLION YOUNG MEN WERE CALLED UP. THEY WERE ENLISTED AS SOON AS THEIR NUMBER CAME UP.

THE ARMY SET UP THIRTY-TWO TRAINING CAMPS. THE RECRUITS NEEDED SIX MONTHS IN THE CAMPS TO BECOME EXPERT SOLDIERS.

SHOULDERS BACK, YOU LOT! YOU'RE IN THE ARMY NOW!

THE FIRST AMERICAN TROOPS TO EMBARK FOR FRANCE WERE 14,500 MEN OF THE MARINES. THE PORTHOLES OF THEIR TROOP SHIPS WERE COVERED BY HATCHES AND THEY SLEPT IN BUNKS FOUR HIGH AGAINST THE SIDES.

SO FAR WE'VE BEEN LIVING AND EATING LIKE CATTLE, BUT THIS IS THE FIRST TIME WE'VE BEEN PENNED IN LIKE SHEEP!

GENERAL JOHN J. PERSHING WAS APPOINTED COMMANDER-IN-CHIEF OF THE AMERICAN EXPEDITIONARY FORCE IN EUROPE. ON THE 4TH OF JULY, HE LAID A WREATH AT THE TOMB OF LAFAYETTE, THE FRENCH GENERAL WHO HAD FOUGHT WITH WASHINGTON IN THE AMERICAN REVOLUTIONARY WAR. PERSHING'S ADJUTANT MADE A SPEECH FOR THE OCCASION.

HERE, IN THE PRESENCE OF OUR GLORIOUS DEAD, WE DECLARE OUR FAITH THAT WE SHALL BRING THIS WAR TO A SUCCESSFUL CONCLUSION. LAFAYETTE... WE HONOUR YOU!

THE HINDENBURG LINE

However, it would be months before the American military forces in France were at full strength. The Germans made the most of this period to reinforce their line of defence on the Western Front.

The Germans decided to retreat some 30 miles and make a new line of trenches.

GENERAL LUDENDORFF... YOU ARE IN CHARGE OF THIS RETREAT!

I SHALL INSTRUCT MY TROOPS IN THAT SECTOR TO DESTROY EVERYTHING THAT COULD BE OF USE TO THE ALLIES!

The new line of defence was the strongest ever established on the Western Front. First, the Germans protected their machine guns by placing them in bunkers*. The Allies called the new German position the Hindenburg Line.

*Fortresses of steel and concrete.

General Nivelle, the hero of Verdun, who had become the new French Commander-in-Chief, positioned his men facing the Hindenburg Line. However, the French were thrown into chaos.

Thousands of French soldiers, shaken by the heavy losses, mutinied or deserted. General Pétain replaced General Nivelle and tried to boost the morale of his men.

IT'S DOWNRIGHT MURDER TO MAKE US FACE THOSE INVULNERABLE BUNKERS!

THAT'S NO LONGER THE CASE. THE FRENCH ARMY IS GOING ON THE DEFENSIVE UNTIL THE AMERICANS HAVE JOINED UP WITH US.

But now the British stood alone on the Western Front. They had to keep the Germans occupied in Flanders whilst the French regrouped their forces.

THE BIGGEST BANG OF THE WAR

British troop movements in Flanders were impeded because the Germans had dug themselves in on the Messines Ridge, just to the south of Ypres. The British had wanted to capture the ridge ever since it had fallen into German hands in 1914.

"General Haig, from that ridge over there the German cannons can shoot us to pieces!"

"The sappers will have to help us!"

The Royal Engineers performed drilling operations in the muddy Flanders top soil and studied the earth samples they had dug up.

"At a depth of 100 feet lies a hard layer of blue clay. We should be able to dig a tunnel through it and plant mines directly under the German positions. However, any digging will take a hell of a long time!"

"Have a go!"

The British chose the southern flank of the ridge for this operation. In 1915, they set to work in the utmost secrecy to dig twenty deep tunnels under the German front line.

For two years, around one thousand men toiled deep underground with pick-axes and shovels. In this way they advanced three to five yards per day!

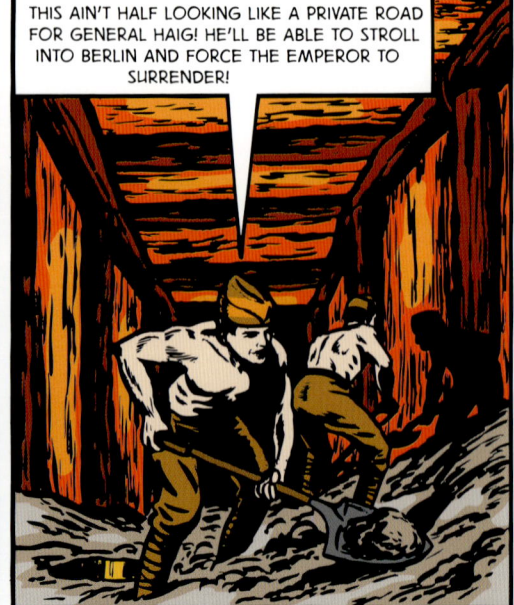

"This ain't half looking like a private road for General Haig! He'll be able to stroll into Berlin and force the Emperor to surrender!"

THE BRITISH DID EVERYTHING THEY COULD TO PREVENT THE GERMANS FROM FINDING OUT ABOUT THEIR TUNNELS. THEY CAMOUFLAGED THE PILES OF BLUE CLAY AND MOVED THEM OFF BEHIND THEIR OWN LINES.

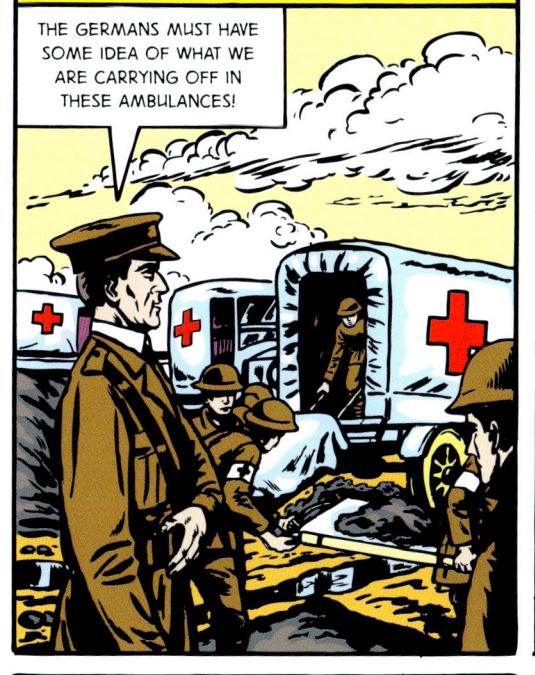

THE GERMANS MUST HAVE SOME IDEA OF WHAT WE ARE CARRYING OFF IN THESE AMBULANCES!

SOME TUNNELS REACHED A LENGTH OF WELL OVER HALF A MILE. WHEN THE TUNNELS WERE FINISHED, THE ENGINEERS PLACED DETONATORS OF A NEW AND PARTICULARLY POWERFUL TYPE AT THE END OF THEM.

CAREFUL, MEN! THERE'S POWERFUL STUFF IN THESE BOXES. WHAT YOU'RE CARRYING COMES TO 100,000 LBS OF DYNAMITE!

BUT AT THAT VERY SAME MOMENT THE GERMANS WERE ALSO BUSY CONSTRUCTING MINE-GALLERIES UNDER THE MESSINES RIDGE. SOMETIMES THE TWO SIDES DUG VERY CLOSE TO EACH OTHER. THEN THE BRITISH HELD THEIR BREATH AND STOOD DEAD STILL!

THE KRAUTS CAN ONLY BE ABOUT A FOOT ABOVE US. EVERYBODY STAND STILL TILL THEY'VE GONE PAST!

AT THE END OF MAY, 1917, THE GERMANS DISCOVERED ONE OF THE BRITISH TUNNELS NEAR MESSINES. THEY BLEW IT UP AND THE BRITISH HAD TO GIVE UP THEIR ATTEMPTS. THE GERMANS SUSPECTED, HOWEVER, THAT THERE WERE MORE TUNNELS.

Panel 1:

After hearing about the mutiny of the French troops in the south, General Haig initiated an attack on the 7th of June, 1917, to open up the German positions at Messines.

"There'd be a catastrophe if the Germans were now to begin an offensive against the French lines. We must keep them busy here in Flanders. There isn't a moment to lose!"

Panel 2:

The Germans heard about the proposed attack from a captured British soldier...

"Bah! This fellow here knows nothing about tunnels. We must send out a patrol to gather earth samples near the British positions. That's the only way to find out if they've been digging near the ridge or not!"

Panel 3:

At the end of May, a German patrol went out to get earth samples.

"Get back! We'll not get through here!"

Panel 4:

The Germans never found the tunnels. On the 30th of May the British barrage began...

"Fire!"

FOR EIGHT DAYS, THE BRITISH CANNONS FIRED HIGH-EXPLOSIVE GAS SHELLS AT THE GERMANS.

"I CAN'T SLEEP WITH THIS AWFUL GAS MASK ON, BUT IT'S TOO DANGEROUS TO TAKE IT OFF!"

"IF I DON'T GET SOME REST BEFORE LONG, I WON'T BE ABLE TO WALK, LET ALONE FIGHT!"

ON THE EVENING OF THE 6TH OF JUNE, BRITISH ENGINEERS TOOK THE DETONATORS INTO THE TUNNELS. A MILLION POUNDS OF HIGH EXPLOSIVE WERE LAID READY TO BE SET OFF AT THE PUSH OF A BUTTON. 80,000 SOLDIERS FROM BRITAIN, AUSTRALIA AND NEW ZEALAND STOOD READY IN THE FORWARD TRENCHES.

"JUST HALF AN HOUR, SERGEANT!"

"SPOT ON, SIR! MEN... GAS MASKS OFF AND BAYONETS READY!"

AT 3:30AM ON THE 7TH OF JUNE, ALL 19 TUNNELS WERE DETONATED. THE MESSINES RIDGE BURST OPEN. COLUMNS OF FIRE REACHED UP INTO THE SKY AND THE NOISE OF THE EXPLOSION WAS HEARD NEARLY 200 MILES AWAY IN LONDON!

Then the British struck up a terrifying artillery barrage. Before long, the British infantry went on the attack.

The blowing-up of the tunnels had gouged out enormous craters in the ridge! Some of these were 30 yards across and 25 deep!

The advancing British came across countless German soldiers in a state of shock.

ROUND THEM ALL UP, MEN. THEY WON'T GIVE ANY TROUBLE. THEY JUST WANT A REST!

The battle for the Messines Ridge was over on the 14th of June. The British front had advanced by more than 2 miles, and the Germans were no longer able to fire on them from the ridge.

YOU CAN SEE ABSOLUTELY EVERYTHING IN YPRES FROM HERE. IT'S NO WONDER WE DIDN'T MAKE ANY HEADWAY!

SLAUGHTER IN THE MUD

Six weeks elapsed between the Battle of the Messines Ridge and the next British offensive. Meanwhile, the Germans set up a strong line of defence. When the British attacked this, on the 31st of July, it was the beginning of the Third Battle of Ypres. By nightfall, the British had gained 200 yards at a cost of 32,000 dead and wounded.

That night the rain began.

The next month was the wettest August in Flanders for 30 years. The ground became a slimy sea of mud. Motorised transport was out of the question.

Hugh Quigley was an infantryman of the 12th Royal Scots Regiment involved in the Third Battle of Ypres.

"Tonight we're going over the top in the middle of this slimy mess. It smells like a muck-heap on a hot day."

The British cannons laid down a terrible barrage and at around 3:30am Quigley's battalion went on the attack.

"Off you go then! Fix bayonets and try to keep your weapons out of the mud!"

WHEN THE WHISTLES WERE BLOWN, QUIGLEY SPRINTED ACROSS NO MAN'S LAND THROUGH THE SHELLS!
A FAST PACE IS COMPLETELY IMPOSSIBLE THROUGH THIS MUD-HEAP. I MUST SEE IF I CAN REACH THE GERMAN TRENCH BEFORE I STOP A BULLET...
QUIGLEY STUMBLED IN THE DARK AND FELL IN A SHELL-CRATER FULL OF STINKING WATER...
I HOPE THE WATER I'VE SWALLOWED WON'T MAKE ME ILL. I COUNT MYSELF LUCKY TO STILL BE ALIVE!
QUIGLEY LAY STILL FOR A WHILE IN THE SHELL-CRATER TO GET HIS BREATH BACK. MACHINE GUN BULLETS SPLATTERED ROUND HIM IN THE WATER. THEN HE SET OFF AGAIN AND LABORIOUSLY REACHED THE GERMAN TRENCH.
I SEE THERE'S NOT MUCH LEFT HERE. OUR ARTILLERY DOESN'T DO THINGS BY HALVES, DOES IT?
SOON, GERMAN SHELLS WERE RAINING DOWN ON THE TRENCH. QUIGLEY AND THE OTHERS STAYED THERE ALL DAY, WAITING FOR THE END OF THE GERMAN BARRAGE.
EVERY TIME ONE OF THOSE THINGS GOES OFF, I GET RAMMED DEEPER INTO THE GROUND. MY WHOLE BODY ACHES!
SO DOES MINE! I'M LYING HERE WITH TREMBLING KNEES. I DON'T THINK I CAN HOLD OUT MUCH LONGER...

THAT NIGHT, QUIGLEY'S UNIT GOT THEIR ORDERS...

WE'VE GOT TO KNOCK OUT THAT GERMAN MACHINE GUN POST OVER THERE. YOU'RE COMING WITH ME, AND BRING SOME GRENADES!

QUIGLEY FOLLOWED HIS SERGEANT AND CLIMBED OUT OF THE TRENCH. THEY CREPT THROUGH THE MUD TOWARDS ONE OF THE BUNKERS.

WHEN WE'RE CLOSE, THROW YOUR HAND GRENADES AT THE WEAPONS SLIT AND RUN!

PRIVATE QUIGLEY TOOK OUT THE PIN AND STEADIED HIMSELF TO AIM AT THE TARGET. AT THAT MOMENT HE WAS HIT BY A BULLET. JUST THEN HIS GRENADE EXPLODED IN THE BUNKER AND KILLED THE MACHINE GUNNERS.

THE SERGEANT REACHED QUIGLEY...

ARE YOU BADLY HURT?

NO, JUST A BULLET IN THE LEG. IT'S THE BEST SORT OF WOUND YOU CAN HAVE, SERGEANT! ONE THAT ALL SOLDIERS PRAY FOR! NOW I CAN GET OUT OF HERE!

NEARLY 250,000 BRITISH SOLDIERS DIED OR WERE WOUNDED IN THIS THIRD BATTLE OF YPRES. THE FIGHTING LASTED FOUR MONTHS AND THE BRITISH ACHIEVED A TERRITORIAL GAIN OF A LITTLE UNDER 5 MILES. HOWEVER, THE FLANDERS OFFENSIVE WAS THE SALVATION OF FRANCE! IT GAVE PÉTAIN ENOUGH TIME TO RESTORE THE MORALE OF HIS TROOPS!

ZEPPELINS AND SAUSAGES

In the Great War, air battles were fought for the first time in history!

At the start of the war, Germany had around 35 motorised metal balloons available; these were known as zeppelins. They could stay in the air for more than 30 hours, and carry two tons of bombs. Some of these zeppelins were almost 500 feet long! In the first year of the war the zeppelins carried out night bombardments on London and Paris. However, the slow and bulky monsters formed a very easy target for the anti-aircraft guns and fighter planes, so it wasn't very long before they disappeared from the scene.

Throughout the war, both sides on the western front made use of observation-balloons. The soldiers nicknamed them sausages. They hung in the air at a height of around 2,000 feet. From baskets underneath the balloons, observers could watch enemy movements over a distance of some fifteen miles. The sausages became the favourite targets of the fighter planes.

THE RED BARON OF GERMANY

The first aircraft used in the war were unsound machines only suitable for observation purposes. Before long, however, better machines were manufactured. These were equipped with heavy machine guns and waged war in the air. The pilots were the knights of the skies.

Manfred von Richthofen was one of the greatest pilots of the war. He began his career as a cavalry officer.

"There's no need for cavalry in this war. That's why we're now sitting here in a trench. The best thing would be sitting up there in a plane!"

Von Richthofen was transferred to the German Air Force, where he was trained as an observer and air-gunner. He flew in a bomber, the Carrier Pigeon.

"Missed again! I don't want to be an air-gunner anymore! I'd rather be a pilot!"

His pilot gave him flying lessons in his free time. Von Richthofen was a slow learner...

"Don't be too down-hearted! Everyone makes a mess of his first land landing!"

"I could kick myself! Will I never learn?"

Von Richthofen failed his first pilot's exam, but he passed the second time and became a bomber pilot!

"That's my first kill! And there's more to come!"

IN SEPTEMBER 1916, ONE OF THE BEST GERMAN PILOTS ASKED VON RICHTHOFEN TO JOIN HIS NEW FIGHTER SQUADRON.

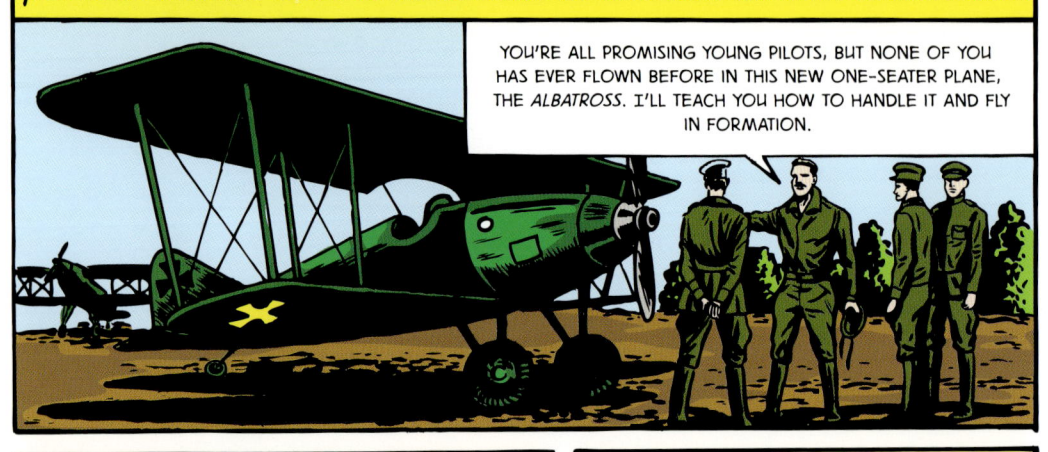

YOU'RE ALL PROMISING YOUNG PILOTS, BUT NONE OF YOU HAS EVER FLOWN BEFORE IN THIS NEW ONE-SEATER PLANE, THE *ALBATROSS*. I'LL TEACH YOU HOW TO HANDLE IT AND FLY IN FORMATION.

AT THE END OF THE MONTH, THE SQUADRON ENGAGED IN BATTLE FOR THE FIRST TIME. VON RICHTHOFEN SHOT DOWN A BRITISH PLANE.

THE PLANE CAME DOWN BEHIND GERMAN LINES. VON RICHTHOFEN LANDED NEARBY AND WAITED TO SEE WHETHER ANY GERMAN SOLDIERS HAD WINESSED HIS VICTORY.

I'M GOING TO BE ONE OF THE BEST PILOTS IN THE GERMAN AIR FORCE!

A MONTH LATER, VON RICHTHOFEN SAW THE CHANCE TO BRING DOWN TWO ENEMY FIGHTERS ON THE SAME DAY!

> A COUPLE OF DAYS LATER, VON RICHTHOFEN EXPERIENCED HIS MOST DIFFICULT DOGFIGHT.

"THE PILOT ON THE RIGHT IS A GOOD FLYER. I'LL GO AND FIGHT IT OUT WITH HIM!"

> THE TWO MACHINES ABANDONED FORMATION AND BEGAN TO CIRCLE EACH OTHER AND LOOP THE LOOP...

> THE BRITISH PILOT MANAGED TO GET BEHIND VON RICHTHOFEN...

"THIS IS GETTING WORRISOME. THIS PILOT KNOWS ALL THE TRICKS OF THE TRADE. I'VE NEVER HAD IT SO DIFFICULT!"

> FINALLY THE BRITISH PLANE RAN OUT OF FUEL. IT QUICKLY FLEW OFF TOWARDS THE BRITISH LINES.

"IF I DON'T GET HIM NOW, I'LL LOSE HIM! IT'S NOW OR NEVER!"

> VON RICHTHOFEN HIT THE BRITISH PLANE. IT SMASHED INTO AN ABANDONED FARMHOUSE IN A BALL OF FLAME A FEW FEET FROM THE GERMAN LINES. TWO DAYS LATER, THE WORLD HEARD THE NEWS THAT VON RICHTHOFEN HAD SHOT DOWN MAJOR L. G. HAWKER, ONE OF AVIATION'S GREATEST MEN!

IN JANUARY 1917, VON RICHTHOFEN WAS GIVEN COMMAND OF HIS OWN SQUADRON. HE HAD HIS OWN PLANE PAINTED RED.

FROM NOW ON EVERY ALLIED PILOT ON THE WESTERN FRONT WILL KNOW WHO HE'S FIGHTING AGAINST.

IN MARCH, VON RICHTHOFEN SHOT DOWN 21 AIRCRAFT. ON THE 29TH OF APRIL, HE ADDED FOUR KILLS TO HIS TOTAL, MAKING IT 52. THE ALLIES CALLED HIM THE RED BARON.

VON RICHTHOFEN TOOK COMMAND OF AN EVEN BIGGER SQUADRON. THIS UNIT WAS SO EFFECTIVE THAT IT BECAME KNOWN AS THE FLYING CIRCUS. HOWEVER ONE DAY, WHEN HE WAS ON PATROL WITH HIS SQUADRON, VON RICHTHOFEN WAS HIMSELF HIT...

I'VE SUDDENLY GONE BLIND! I MUST MAKE SURE I DON'T LOSE CONTROL! IF I CAN JUST REACH MY OWN LINES!

VON RICHTHOFEN LANDED SAFELY AND HE WAS SOON BACK IN THE AIR. FOR EVERY TIME HE SHOT DOWN AN ENEMY AIRCRAFT, HE ORDERED A LITTLE SILVER CUP ON WHICH HIS VICTORY WAS INSCRIBED. AT THE END OF 1917, 63 SILVER TROPHIES DECORATED HIS BOOKSHELVES!

DURING THE GERMAN CAMPAIGN OF 1918, VON RICHTHOFEN WAS MAKING AN AVERAGE 5 PATROLS PER DAY. ON THE 20TH OF APRIL, TWO SHOT-DOWN AIRCRAFT BROUGHT HIS TOTAL UP TO 80. OF ALL WAR-TIME PILOTS HE WAS THE ONE WITH THE GREATEST NUMBER OF KILLS.
CONGRATULATIONS, CAPTAIN VON RICHTHOFEN!
MANFRED, YOU'RE THE BEST OF THE LOT! THIS EVENING WE'LL CELEBRATE WITH CHAMPAGNE!
THE NEXT DAY, WHILE VON RICHTHOFEN PREPARED AGAIN FOR TAKE-OFF, A PHOTOGRAPHER DASHED ON TO THE AIRFIELD TO CAPTURE HIM FOR POSTERITY.
HEY, HAVE YOU GONE CRAZY? PHOTOGRAPHING A PILOT BEFORE TAKE-OFF BRINGS BAD LUCK!
RUBBISH! I DON'T BELIEVE IN SUPERSTITIOUS NONSENSE!
THE FLYING CIRCUS HAD ONLY BEEN IN THE AIR A COUPLE OF MINUTES WHEN IT WAS ATTACKED BY A SQUADRON OF BRITISH FIGHTERS. WHILE VON RICHTHOFEN WAS ENGAGING ONE OF THE ENEMY, ANOTHER BRITISH PLANE DIVED ABOVE HIM.
THE RED PLANE DIVED DOWN.
IT LANDED UNDAMAGED BEHIND THE BRITISH LINES.
IT'S VON RICHTHOFEN... HE'S DEAD!

THE DOWNFALL OF TWO NATIONS

In the autumn of 1917, Germany discovered that two of her enemies were out of the conflict.

Italy, which originally formed part of the Central European Alliance, was still relatively neutral in 1914. The Italian people showed no interest in the war. However, some of their leaders saw the opportunity to increase Italy's power through the conflict. In April 1915, Italy made a secret agreement with the Allies in which great territorial gains were promised in exchange for an Italian attack on Austria. From May 1915 to October 1917, Italian and Austrian troops stood silently facing each other on a 60-mile front along the Isonzo river. For Italy, this episode ended on the 24th of October, 1917, when German and Austrian troops broke through this front at the town of Caporetto. In two months, the Italian army lost over 600,000 men. Though Italy did not surrender, she could do little for the Allies for the rest of the war.

Without help from the West, the Russian war effort was doomed to failure. Around September 1916, Russia had had to abandon the whole of Poland and Lithuania. Russian losses ran into the millions. The people were unhappy and rebellion broke out in St. Petersburg, in the Ukraine and in many other places in Russia too. On the 7th of November, 1917, the Communist Party came to power under Vladimir Lenin. Germany immediately offered the Russians an armistice. Large sections of the old Russian Empire were yielded to Germany and on the 15th of December, 1917, the war on the Eastern Front drew to a close.

THE LAST ADVANCE

After the war on the Eastern Front was over, Germany was able to transfer 1.5 million soldiers to the West. For the first time in the war she had a greater number of troops than the Allies.

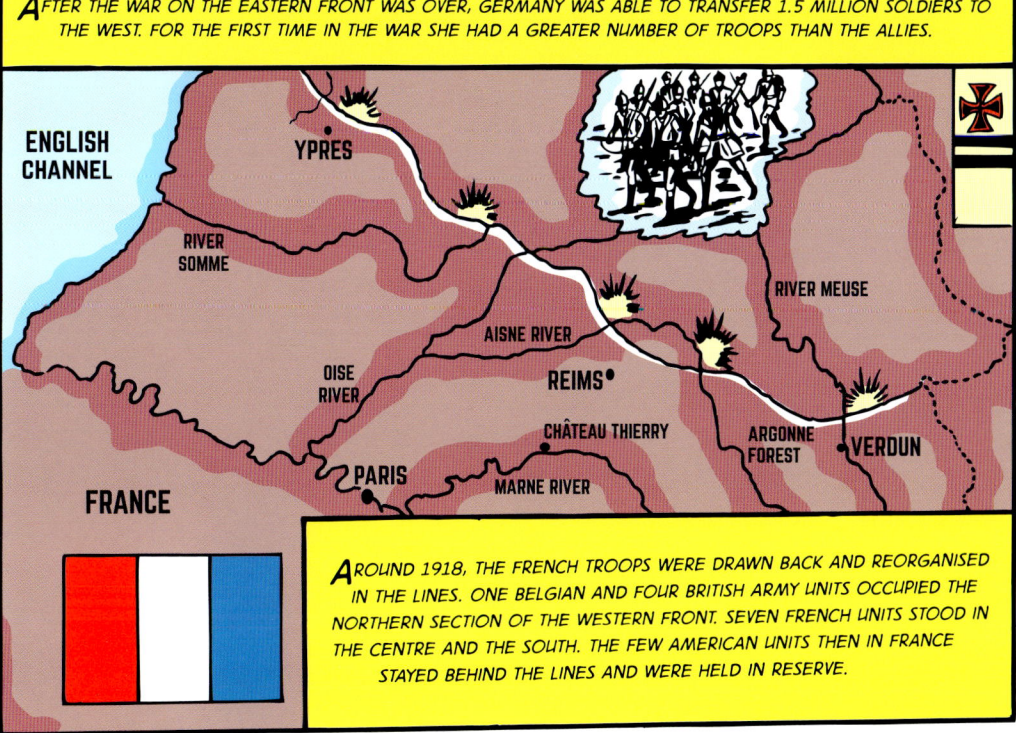

Around 1918, the French troops were drawn back and reorganised in the lines. One Belgian and four British army units occupied the northern section of the Western Front. Seven French units stood in the centre and the south. The few American units then in France stayed behind the lines and were held in reserve.

German strategists decided to attack the 50-mile section of the front where the British and French sectors met.

We shall drive a wedge between the French and the British and cut them off from each other. Then we'll be able to defeat them separately. We must get it done before the Americans reach full strength!

The Germans took great pains to move their troops without being seen.

If you men have finished covering up the tyres, you can begin camouflaging the camp!

On the 21st of March, 1918, at around 4:30am, 43 divisions went on the attack, taking the Allies by surprise. For five hours gas-grenades and other explosives rained down on the British. Then the German infantry advanced.

The British lost contact with the French on their right flank and they were soon in full retreat. The Germans crossed the Somme and established a bridgehead on the south bank.

On the 23rd of March, the Germans started to bombard Paris with three unprecedented huge cannons, which had been placed under cover 80 miles away in a wood. The Allies called these cannons "Big Berthas".*

*"Big Berthas" may have been named after Bertha Krupp, owner of the Krupp Armaments Manufacturing Company.

Then the Germans tried to conquer Amiens, a city on the Somme, some 70 miles from Paris. However, the British managed to re-establish contact with the French, and threw their reserves into battle. After 2 weeks' fighting, Amiens was once again in Allied hands.

Heavy losses forced General Ludendorff to abandon the attack on Amiens. The Germans were pushed back about 30 miles, so they failed to separate the Allied armies from each other.

THE GERMANS NOW TURNED AGAINST THE BRITISH IN FLANDERS IN THE HOPE OF REACHING THE FRENCH CHANNEL PORTS. SHOULD THIS FAIL, THEY THEN INTENDED TO TRY AND GET HOLD OF THE IMPORTANT RAILWAY JUNCTION AT HAZEBROUCK, 15 MILES SOUTH OF YPRES.

EARLY IN THE MORNING OF THE 9TH OF APRIL, 14 GERMAN DIVISIONS ATTACKED OVER A FRONT 12 MILES IN LENGTH. THEY MADE A BREACH IN THE LINES AND POURED THROUGH.

ON THE 12TH OF APRIL, THE GERMANS STOOD JUST OVER 4 MILES FROM HAZEBROUCK. THE BRITISH POSITION WAS UNTENABLE... GENERAL HAIG'S ORDER OF THE DAY WAS READ OUT EVERYWHERE TO THE MEN BY THEIR OFFICERS...

NOW WE'VE GOT OUR BACKS TO THE WALL, I EXPECT EVERY MAN TO FIGHT TO THE END. AT THIS CRITICAL MOMENT, THE FREEDOM OF MANKIND HANGS ON THE INDIVIDUAL CONDUCT OF EACH ONE OF US!

THEN, THE GERMANS SHIFTED THE FOCAL POINT OF THEIR OFFENSIVE TO THE NORTH. ON THE 16TH OF APRIL, THEY TOOK THE MESSINES RIDGE. WITH A HEAVY HEART THE BRITISH GAVE UP THIS TERRITORY WHICH HAD COST THEM SO MUCH EFFORT TO CONQUER.

AT LEAST 250,000 BRITISH SOLDIERS WILL TURN IN THEIR GRAVES BECAUSE OF THIS!

FRENCH RESERVE TROOPS QUICKLY RUSHED TO HELP THE EXHAUSTED BRITISH SOLDIERS. THE FIGHTING SHIFTED TOWARDS KEMELBERG, A HILL TO THE SOUTH OF YPRES. THE GERMANS WERE REPELLED THERE BY THE BRITISH AND FRENCH, SO THE ALLIED RESISTANCE WAS ABLE TO PREVENT THE GERMANS FROM REACHING HAZEBROUCK OR THE OTHER FRENCH CHANNEL PORTS.

On the 14th of April, Marshal Ferdinand Foch was appointed Commander-in-Chief of the Allied Armed Forces in the West. Generals Haig, Pétain and Pershing formed part of his staff. For the first time in the war the Allies had a joint supreme command.

On the 27th of May, the Germans struck for the third time!

"We're going to give the French the coup de grâce, now that a number of their troops have joined up with the British in Flanders. We shall attack along the river Aisne!"

In the morning, the Germans drove the French from the hilltops to the north of Aisne.

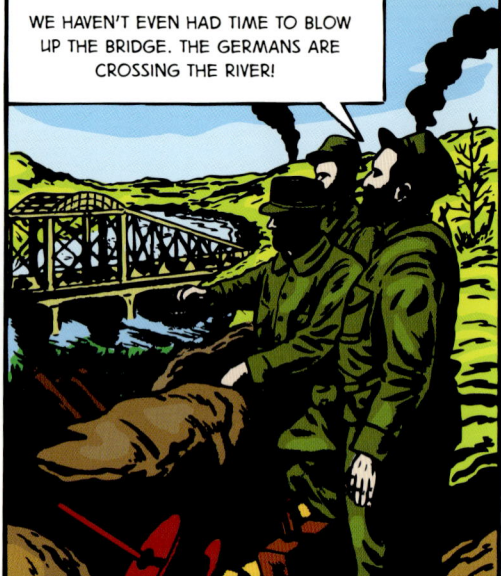

"We haven't even had time to blow up the bridge. The Germans are crossing the river!"

In the next couple of days the Germans tried to widen the new salient they had made in the enemy lines. To the south of Aisne, they pushed along towards Rheims in the west, and in an easterly direction towards Soissons. Marshal Foch was determined to hold them back.

"If we can prevent the Germans from taking Rheims and Soissons, we'll be able to cut off and surround their salient."

However, Soissons fell on the 29th of May.

TWO DAYS LATER, THE ADVANCED UNITS REACHED THE NORTH BANK OF THE MARNE. AT CHÂTEAU-THIERRY, THEY WAITED FOR THE MAIN BODY OF THE ARMY TO CATCH UP WITH THEM. THE ROAD TO PARIS LAY ON THE OPPOSITE SIDE OF THE RIVER. THE FRENCH CAPITAL LAY NO MORE THAN 50 MILES AWAY. VICTORY SEEMED CLOSE AT HAND.
PARIS 35 KM
HOWEVER, FRENCH AND AMERICAN REINFORCEMENTS WERE ON THE WAY. IN MAY 1918, 300,000 AMERICAN SOLDIERS LANDED IN FRANCE.
LONG LIVE THE YANKS!
U.S.M.C.
THE GERMANS TRIED TO CROSS THE MARNE AT CHÂTEAU-THIERRY. HOWEVER, IN THE MEANTIME, AMERICAN TROOPS HAD ARRIVED...
...TO DEFEND THE BRIDGES! OTHER US TROOPS SPREAD THEMSELVES ALONG THE MAIN ROAD TO PARIS, TO THE SOUTH-WEST OF CHÂTEAU-THIERRY. SIDE BY SIDE WITH THE FRENCH UNITS, THEY GOT READY TO STAVE OFF THE GERMAN ADVANCE ON PARIS.
THE GERMANS COULD NOT ADVANCE FURTHER WITHOUT REPLENISHING SUPPLIES. ON THE 3RD OF JUNE, THEIR THIRD OFFENSIVE CAME TO AN END. AGAIN THEY TRIED TO WIDEN THEIR SALIENT THROUGH A FOURTH ATTACK FURTHER TO THE WEST, BUT THIS FAILED.

BRIDGEHEAD OVER THE MARNE

Germany lost her numerical advantage when more and more American soldiers began to arrive in France. However, she still had enough time and military strength for another offensive.

General Ludendorff transported men and equipment from every possible sector of the front. The German troops began to move in from both the east and west of Rheims.

"WE SHALL AGAIN ENGAGE IN BATTLE ALONG THE MARNE AND SO REACH PARIS!"

On the 15th of July, just after midnight, the German bombardment began. It rained down upon trenches that were almost empty – the Allies had thinned out their forward positions and were now planning to counterattack from their second lines.

To the Germans' great surprise, the Allies replied to their bombardment with a barrage of their own.

The Germans were utterly unable to penetrate the Allies' second line of defence. After heavy losses they were forced to retreat. The German attempt to conquer Rheims from the east was a failure!

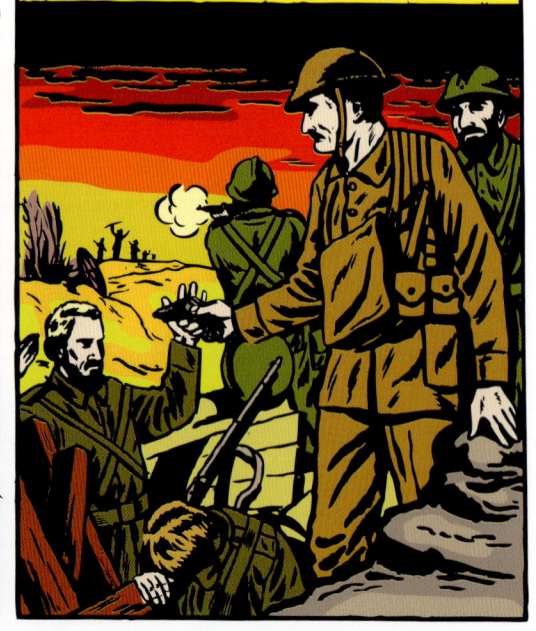

Whilst some German army units attacked Rheims from the east, others made an offensive against the city from the west. Among them was the Second Battalion of the Fifth Grenadiers, under the command of Lieutenant Kurt Hesse. It was Hesse who spoke to his sergeant...	I hope that the spotter planes up there haven't noticed the boats we'll be using to cross the river.

"Allied planes have been flying over us all day..."

"Planes always make me nervous. Even when you take cover, you still get the feeling that they've got you in their sights!"

When the Fifth Grenadiers reached their positions in a wood about half a mile from the Marne, Lieutenant Hesse ordered his men to halt.

"Tell your men to hide the boats under the brushwood until it's time to go to the river."

The Germans were busy setting up their equipment in the wood when they came under fire from the enemy artillery.

"SHELLS! TAKE COVER!"

81

LIEUTENANT HESSE LED HIS BATTALION OUT OF THE WOOD AND TOWARDS THE RIVER BANK. THEY HAD TAKEN THE BOATS WITH THEM. HOWEVER, SHELLS WERE STILL RAINING DOWN ON THEM.
WE'LL GET ACROSS HERE!
ON THE 15TH OF JULY, FROM MIDDAY TILL 1PM, THE FIFTH GRENADIERS BEGAN TO CROSS THE MARNE. LIEUTENANT HESSE WAS IN THE FIRST BOAT.
WHEN WE'RE ACROSS WE'LL CAPTURE THE RAILWAY STATION. THEN WE'LL HEAD SOUTH AND JOIN UP WITH THE OTHER UNITS.
HALF WAY ACROSS THE RIVER, LIEUTENANT HESSE'S BOAT CAME UNDER ENEMY MACHINE GUN FIRE.
WHY HAVEN'T OUR ARTILLERY KNOCKED OUT THE MACHINE GUN NESTS?
WATCH OUT!
NEVERTHELESS, ALL THE GERMAN BOATS GOT SAFELY TO THE OTHER SIDE. HOWEVER, THE SOUTH BANK OF THE MARNE WAS STEEPER THAN EXPECTED.
PULL YOURSELVES UP ON THE WILLOW BRANCHES, BUT KEEP YOUR HEADS DOWN AND LOOK OUT FOR BARBED WIRE!

FRENCH TROOPS WERE OCCUPYING A TRENCH JUST BEHIND THE RIVER BANK. THE GERMANS SPRANG IN AND CAPTURED THE POSITIONS.

AFTER A SHORT STRUGGLE, THE GERMANS ALSO TOOK THE RAILWAY STATION.

THEN THEY MARCHED SOUTH THROUGH AN AREA OF LAND COVERED IN TALL GRASS. SUDDENLY THEY HEARD SHOUTS AND WERE ATTACKED BY AMERICAN SOLDIERS.

THE AMERICANS PUT A STOP TO THE PROGRESS OF LIEUTENANT HESSE'S UNIT.

SERGEANT, TELL THE MEN TO WITHDRAW TO THE STATION AND WAIT THERE. I'LL SEND A RUNNER BACK OVER THE RIVER REQUESTING REINFORCEMENTS. AS SOON AS WE'VE GOT MACHINE GUNS WE'LL BE ABLE TO DEAL WITH THESE AMERICANS!

BUT HESSE NEVER SAW HIS REINFORCEMENTS. ALLIED BOMBERS ANNIHILATED THE GERMAN SUPPLY LINES NEAR THE MARNE. THE FIFTH GRENADIERS BEAT A RETREAT!

Soon after, the other German troops were also forced to abandon their bridgehead over the Marne. On the 21st of July the Allies crossed the river and took control of Château-Thierry.

Ludendorff now threw his best troops into battle. While the Allies advanced north, the German rear-guard was protected by the elite troops of the Prussian Guard. The towns on the front line were continually changing hands.

However, on the 3rd of August, the German resistance crumbled. The Allies took Soissons. The following day they took more than thirty of the neighbouring villages.

Three days later, the German salient over the Marne was nothing but a memory. The Germans had lost 168,000 men, more than they could replace. The Second Battle of the Marne, just like the first, had turned into a German defeat.

THE FINAL BLOW

Between the 8th of August and the end of September, the Allied armies pushed the Germans back behind the Hindenburg Line with a number of storming attacks.

To the east of Amiens, the Allies secretly assembled nine tank battalions and more than 2,000 cannons. On the 8th of August, 450 tanks rumbled through thick mist towards the German lines. Utterly confounded, the Germans took to their heels.

Before long, Allied heavy armoured cars were hunting behind the German lines. On the first day, the Allies gained five miles of territory.

Ludendorff believed that the 8th of August was the blackest day in German military history.

Not only have six or seven of our divisions been wiped out, but also the fighting spirit of all our armed forces has been extinguished. What concerns me is that for Germany, the war may be lost!

The offensive on the Somme finished on the 12th of August. Then, the Allies gathered their forces for the final attack.

IN MID-SEPTEMBER, MARSHAL FOCH HELD A CONFERENCE WITH THE ALLIED COMMANDERS.

WE MUST NOW ELIMINATE GERMANY'S FINAL RESERVES. A COMBINED ALLIED OFFENSIVE WILL BE PRECEDED BY AN AMERICAN ATTACK IN THE SECTOR BETWEEN THE MEUSE AND THE FOREST OF ARGONNE.

THE AMERICAN FRONT WAS 23 MILES WIDE. IT WAS BOUNDED ON THE EAST BY THE RIVER MEUSE AND IN THE WEST BY THE THICKLY WOODED AREA AROUND ARGONNE. IT WAS AN EXCEEDINGLY DIFFICULT PLACE FOR FIGHTING. ON THE EVE OF THE ATTACK, AMERICAN TROOPS QUIETLY REPLACED THE FRENCH, WHO HAD BEEN POSITIONED ALONG THE FRONT FOR 4 YEARS.

SEE YOU, YANK! WATCH OUT FOR GERMAN GUNNERS! MAKE SURE YOU SIT BEHIND TREES AND BOULDERS!

GENERAL PERSHING ASSEMBLED HIS DIVISIONAL COMMANDERS...

OUR TARGET IS THE RAILWAY LINE AT SEDAN, ABOUT 30 MILES FURTHER ON! THIS LINE IS THE MAIN ARTERY OF THE WHOLE GERMAN ARMY IN FRANCE. YOUR ORDERS ARE AS FOLLOWS: SEIZE THE ARTERY... AND CUT THROUGH IT!

ON THE 26TH OF SEPTEMBER, SEVEN AMERICAN DIVISIONS BEGAN TO MOVE. THE MAJORITY OF THE AMERICANS WERE SEEING ACTION FOR THE FIRST TIME IN THEIR LIVES.

HIT THE GERMANS WITH EVERYTHING YOU'VE GOT. AND REMEMBER... TONIGHT WE'RE ALL SEASONED FIGHTERS!

ON THE 11TH OF OCTOBER, THE AMERICAN TROOPS STUMBLED UPON A GERMAN DEFENCE LINE RECKONED TO BE THE STRONGEST. THIS WAS THE KRIEMHILDE LINE, A NETWORK OF BUNKERS AND TRENCHES PLACED DIAGONALLY THROUGH THE FOREST OF ARGONNE.

THE LOST BATTALION

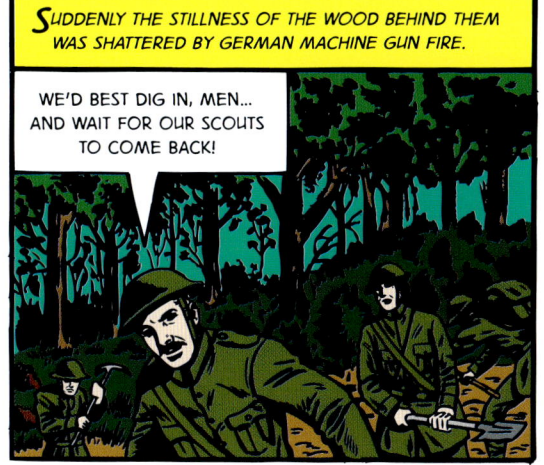

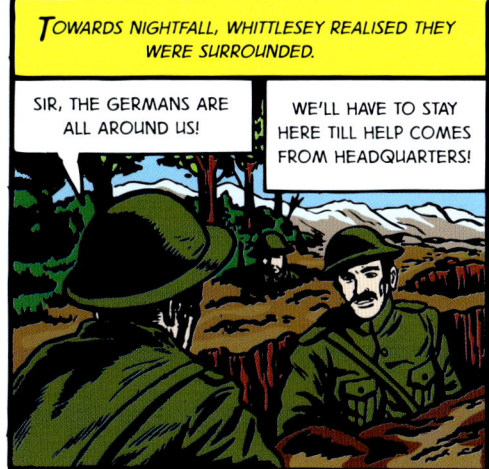

During the offensive, only a small number of Americans fought in the Forest of Argonne. On the 4th of October, the 77th Division got orders to dislodge the Germans. The First Battalion of the 308th Infantry Regiment, under the command of Major Charles Whittlesey, was to prepare for the operation.

Whittlesey's men moved fast. They disappeared over Hill 198 and into the next valley. But then Major Whittlesey began to get anxious.

"Something tells me we're not on the right track. I'm asking four volunteers to go and find out what's going on!"

Suddenly the stillness of the wood behind them was shattered by German machine gun fire.

"We'd best dig in, men... and wait for our scouts to come back!"

Towards nightfall, Whittlesey realised they were surrounded.

"Sir, the Germans are all around us!"

"We'll have to stay here till help comes from headquarters!"

IN THE EVENING, WHITTLESEY'S MEN DUG THEMSELVES INTO FOXHOLES AND WAITED FOR SOMETHING TO HAPPEN...
THERE ARE 575 OF US... I HOPE THAT'LL BE ENOUGH TO HOLD BACK THE GERMANS UNTIL HELP COMES. THERE'S NO WAY OF KNOWING HOW LONG WE'LL HAVE TO STAY HERE!
THE NEXT DAY, THE GERMANS HARASSED THE AMERICAN BATTALION WITH HEAVY SHELLFIRE.
ON THE THIRD DAY, AN AMERICAN PILOT SAW WHERE THE GERMAN CANNON FIRE WAS COMING FROM AND DROPPED A VERY LIGHT ON THE SPOT TO SHOW THE AMERICAN ARTILLERY WHERE TO SHOOT.
THOSE MUST BE THE CANNONS WHICH ARE FIRING ON OUR 1ST BATTALION. OUR ARTILLERY CAN NOW TARGET THE FLARE AND SILENCE THE GERMANS!
HOWEVER, THE AMERICAN GUNNERS MISCALCULATED THE DISTANCE.
THOSE ARE OUR SHELLS! I CAN TELL BY THE SOUND! THEY'LL HAVE TO STOP FIRING!

For four hours, the men of the 1st Battalion were exposed to shellfire from their own artillery! Major Whittlesey tried to send a messenger to headquarters.

This is our last carrier pigeon, sir! His name is Cher Ami... which means "Dear Friend".

Well, dear friend... fly back to headquarters and tell them to stop slaughtering us here!

The message reached its target. However, the 1st Battalion was in the Forest of Argonne for five whole days, and only 275 of them survived, desperate for food and water. Allied planes flew over low and dropped food parcels, the majority of which fell way off target.

Don't bother! Just give me five water-bottles, and I'll try and find water somewhere...

Early in the morning of the sixth day, three men were on their way hoping to convey a message. At midday two of them returned...

We didn't manage it, sir... and the third man is dead...

On the 10th of October, an infantry battalion was advancing along the edge of the wood towards the north. In the evening, they met up with Major Whittlesey and his men, who had appeared out of the woods. After this, they were relieved by another battalion.

So, you're the so-called "Lost Battalion"?

Not exactly lost! We were surrounded, that's all!

Major Whittlesey was promoted for his courage and awarded the Medal of Honor, the highest American military decoration.

JUST LIKE A SQUIRREL HUNT

The Americans were also in action elsewhere in the Forest of Argonne. On the 8th of October, "G" Company of the 82nd Division received orders to march.

We've got to capture that valley down there and the railway two miles further on. Check your watches. Tomorrow morning at 6:10am we'll be on our way!

At the agreed time, the men fixed their bayonets and stormed out of the trenches. One of the soldiers was Corporal Alvin C. York, from the mountain state of Tennessee.

Whilst they were threading their way through the valley, German machine guns opened fire. Corporal York fell down to avoid the bullets.

I reckon all the machine guns in the German army are pointing at us!

York's platoon commander, a sergeant, yelled an order at him...

York, take your patrol and silence that machine gun!

CORPORAL YORK BECKONED HIS MEN. THEY STORMED FORWARD THROUGH THE WOOD...

FOLLOW ME!

THE BEST THING WOULD BE TO WORK OUR WAY THROUGH THE BUSHES AND ATTACK THE GERMANS FROM BEHIND. STAY IN SINGLE FILE AND KEEP UNDER COVER! AND REMEMBER: NO NOISE!

THE PATROL EMERGED BEHIND A GROUP OF TWENTY-FIVE GERMAN SOLDIERS UNDER THE COMMAND OF A MAJOR. YORK AND HIS MEN TOOK THEM PRISONER.

AT THAT VERY MOMENT THE WHOLE GROUP CAME UNDER GERMAN MACHINE GUN FIRE. EVERYONE THREW THEMSELVES FLAT ON THE GROUND. CORPORAL YORK WAS SURPRISED THAT HE HAD BEEN SPOTTED.

WE'RE STUCK HERE BEHIND THE GUNNERS... THEY MUST HAVE SHIFTED ROUND!

AND IF THEY WANT TO GET US IN THEIR SIGHTS, THEY'RE GOING TO HAVE TO POKE THEIR HEADS UP. EVERY TIME ONE OF THEM MAKES A MOVE, I'LL DRAW A BEAD ON HIM, JUST LIKE SQUIRREL HUNTING BACK HOME!

While York was busy knocking off the gunners one by one, a German officer and five soldiers leapt out of their trenches and ran at him. York carried on firing, and when he ran out of cartridges he pulled out his .45 calibre automatic pistol.

The German major crept up to York on his stomach and said to him in English...

You've killed quite enough Germans now. If you stop shooting, I'll guarantee that our machine gunners surrender!

York pointed his gun at the major, but did not fire. The major blew his whistle and shouted something in German to his marksmen. About 50 German soldiers clambered out of their trenches and stood there a while with their hands up.

Corporal York took about 80 German prisoners. He had killed 25. But only 8 of his own patrol were still alive.

We must get the Germans away from here. Get them into line with the major at the front. I'll walk behind and keep an eye on them. You spread out and watch the spaces on our flanks and behind us!

Then York came upon a couple of wounded Americans. He called the column to a halt. Major... tell your men to carry these wounded soldiers!	**Then the double file got going again towards the American lines.** Major, we'll soon be going right through the German positions. Every time we reach a German machine gun post, blow your whistle and tell your gunners to surrender. If you don't, I'll start shooting straight away... and you'll be first!
Eventually York reached his headquarters... Corporal York... I hear you've taken prisoner all the Germans in the Forest of Argonne! Not all of them, sir! Just 132 officers and men!	**General Pershing named Corporal York as the greatest soldier of the whole war. York was promoted to sergeant, and he won the Medal of Honor and a great number of foreign decorations.**

SURRENDER

The Allied advance continued. On the 1st of November, 1918, they drove the Germans almost completely out of French territory.

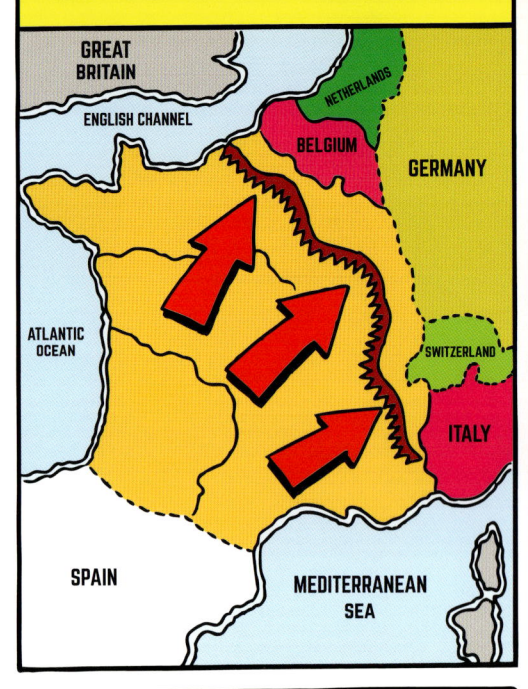

The American army eventually forced a breakthrough in the Kriemhilde Line. It rained almost every day, but on the 6th of November, the American units captured the extremely important German railway at Sedan.

On the same day, Germany assembled a delegation for a meeting with Marshal Foch and was informed of the Allied conditions for an armistice. No military representatives were included in the German delegation.

We shall only delegate civil authorities for the signing of the armistice. The shame of surrender must not come down upon the German General Staff!

On the 8th of November, the German negotiating team was escorted to Marshal Foch's headquarters in a railway carriage in the Forest of Compiègne.

GERMANY HAD NO OTHER CHOICE THAN TO SURRENDER. AUSTRIA HAD ALREADY CAPITULATED ON THE 3RD OF NOVEMBER, AND IN MUNICH AND OTHER GERMAN CITIES RIOTS BROKE OUT. THE GERMAN EMPEROR, KAISER WILHELM II, FLED TO HOLLAND.

AT 5:30AM ON THE 11TH OF NOVEMBER, 1918, THE LEADER OF THE GERMAN DELEGATION SIGNED THE ARMISTICE AGREEMENT.

MARSHAL FOCH ORDERED THE ALLIED TROOPS TO CEASE FIRE. ON THAT DAY AT 11:00AM, AN EERIE, ALMOST MOURNFUL SILENCE FELL OVER THE WESTERN FRONT. THE MEN CAME OUT OF THEIR TRENCHES.

AND I'M STILL ALIVE!

THE GREAT WAR WAS OVER. IN ALLIED COUNTRIES, WILD PARTIES BROKE OUT.

OF THE 60 MILLION SOLDIERS WHO HAD FOUGHT IN THE GREAT WAR, 8 MILLION HAD FALLEN AND 30 MILLION OTHERS WERE WOUNDED OR MISSING. THE EUROPEANS BEGAN TO REBUILD THEIR RUINED WORLD. THE FIRST STEP TOWARDS THIS WAS THE DRAFTING OF A PEACE TREATY...

THE TREATY OF VERSAILLES

After the war, in 1919, the Allied leaders met in Versailles to hammer out the peace treaty. There were no German representatives present throughout this process. President Wilson of the United States wanted a treaty which would guarantee the safety and independence of the European minority groups. He hoped for the establishment of an international organisation which would resolve disputes between countries without resorting to weapons.

However, Britain (David Lloyd George), France (Georges Clemenceau) and Italy (Vittorio Emanuele Orlando) decided that the most important element of a peace treaty should be to punish Germany. They considered that Germany had started the war and wished to safeguard against any possible German aggression in the future.

The Treaty of Versailles did indeed give rise to an international organisation: the League of Nations. However, this had little authority owing to the refusal of America to join. President Wilson was unable to convince the American Congress that the United States should get closely involved in European affairs.

Germany was punished! She lost her colonies and her battle fleet. Her army was restricted to no more than 100,000 men and she had to pay reparations for all damage caused to civilian populations by the war – a cost amounting to £6.6 billion (roughly equivalent to £284 billion today!)

New countries were formed. The oppressed minorities of the former Austrian Empire and Russia got their independence. The map of Europe had to be redrawn and new countries appeared: Yugoslavia, Czechoslovakia, Finland, Poland, Estonia, Latvia and Lithuania. But the old disputes lingered on. Neither the war, nor the treaty, were able to bring to an end the fear...

...and the envy between the different countries. The treaty, which brought to an end the First World War, was the cause of friction which would eventually give rise, a mere 20 years later, to **THE SECOND WORLD WAR!**

World War I: *Introduction*

by William B. Jones, Jr.

The First World War was a human catastrophe of unprecedented proportions. It was also a horrific accretion of ironies perhaps best encapsulated in the name originally given the conflict - the "Great War". "Every war constitutes an irony of situation because its means are so melodramatically disproportionate to its presumed ends," Paul Fussell has observed. "In the Great War eight million people were destroyed because two persons, the Archduke ... and his Consort, had been shot. ... [T]he Great War was more ironic than any before or since. ... It reversed the Idea of Progress" (Fussell 8). Military historian John Keegan asserts that "it damaged civilisation, the rational and liberal civilisation of the European Enlightenment, permanently for the worse and, through the damage done, world civilisation also" (Keegan 8).

From 1815 to 1914, Europe had known an era of peace punctuated by brief, limited hostilities such as the Crimean War and the Franco-Prussian War. Late 19th century advances in science, medicine, and technology gave rise to the generally held notion that the lot of humankind was steadily, irreversibly improving. Of course, there had been nationalist, socialist, or anarchist stirrings on the continent, and political assassinations here and there. But on the whole, things seemed to most Europeans as right as right could be. Then, on 28th June 1914, the Austrian Archduke Franz Ferdinand, heir presumptive to the throne, and his lower-ranking wife paid a public-relations visit to Sarajevo, capital of the Austro-Hungarian province of Bosnia-Herzegovina, where they were assassinated by Serbian nationalist Gavrilo Princip. This act set in motion a domino chain-effect of interlocking alliances (Austria-Hungary and Germany; Russia, Serbia, and France; Great Britain and Belgium) that led to a war no one particularly wanted to fight.

That summer - the summer of 1914 - was the loveliest that anyone in Europe could recall, or so everyone in Europe seemed to agree in retrospect. Perhaps it was an understandable human longing for some ideal of perfection to stand in contrast to the four years of horror that followed. But the idea of a future European war had been in the air for years. Books had been written about a coming conflict, including Friedrich von Bernhardi's *Germany and the Next War* (1912). In the same year, the final touches were put on an attack strategy devised nearly a decade earlier by the former Chief of the German General Staff, Alfred von Schlieffen, whose plan called for the German army to sweep from the north through Belgium into France and on to Paris and victory in six weeks. With the French out of the way, the Germans could then turn their attention eastward to the Russians. But geography and other nations' mobilisation efforts proved to be complicating factors. The Battle of the Marne and the Race to the Sea changed the landscape of the Western Front, thwarting the Schlieffen Plan and turning the conflict into trench warfare stretching from the Swiss border to the North Sea.

Hostilities spread worldwide, from Gallipoli to the Pacific. New or improved technology brought hitherto unknown means of killing to wartime experience, from the airplane to the tank. The bombing of civilian centres by Zeppelins and the sinking of passenger ships such as the *Lusitania* provoked outrage. But the horrors of the First World War weren't inflicted exclusively by means of modern machinery. As it advanced

1917 - Canadian troops with a British Mark II Tank at the Battle of Vimy Ridge

through Belgium, in clear violation of its neutrality, the German army **Cont'd** engaged in atrocities against civilians on a stunning scale. For example, in August 1914, panicked German troops in the university city of Louvain, believing they were being attacked by snipers, went on a three-day burning and killing spree that resulted in the destruction of more than 1,000 buildings (including one-fifth of the houses) and a library of 230,000 books and medieval manuscripts. More than 200 civilians were killed and 42,000 forcibly evacuated. The civilian death toll in other Belgian towns was comparable or worse: German troops shot 211 at Andenne, 384 at Tamines, and 612 at Dinant. These numbers included men, women, and children. (Gilbert 42-43; Keegan 82-3; Kramer 1-24.) The resulting British propaganda depicting "the rape of Belgium" was undoubtedly lurid and shrill but certainly not entirely overstated.

Still, it was the combatants on both sides in the Great War who bore the greatest part of death and suffering as the seemingly endless conflict continued month after month, year after year. On the Western Front, the same terrain was fought over, with little to show for all the losses in the end. "From the winter of 1914 until the spring of 1918 the trench system was fixed, moving here and there a few hundred yards, moving on great occasions as much as a few miles" (Fussell 36). Mud, barbed wire, and trenchfoot were daily realities, punctuated by the terrors summed up in the names Ypres, Verdun, and the Argonne Forest. But of all the episodes of the First World War, the one that endures as a symbol of senseless slaughter is the first day of the Battle of the Somme, 1st July 1916. That morning, before the British and French troops launched their attack, about 250,000 shells were fired at the German line, while ten mines beneath the German trenches were exploded. Within minutes, British and French soldiers began advancing in high spirits, feeling certain that the enemy positions had been softened up. Some British battalions kicked footballs ahead of them. But the men were weighed down with sixty-six pounds of equipment, and they gathered in groups to deal with the uncut barbed wire they encountered in No Man's Land. Meanwhile, German troops, who had been safely hidden in their better-constructed trenches, retrieved their machine guns, set them up, and began mowing down the slowly moving British soldiers.

Vickers Machine Gun

The carnage was so appalling that many of the Germans stopped firing to allow the wounded to retreat. It was the bloodiest day in British military history. (Gilbert 258-259; Keegan 294-296; Stokesbury 152-153.)

According to historian John Keegan, "The Somme marked the end of an age of vital optimism in British life that has never been recovered" (Keegan 299). Indeed, the Western world, from Europe to America and beyond, never quite got over the sense of disillusionment that settled in. The habit of distrust of political and religious leaders came naturally to those who believed they had been deceived and betrayed by them. Soldier-poets such as Wilfred Owen (*Anthem for Doomed Youth*) and Siegfried Sassoon (*Does It Matter?*) expressed a bitterly ironical cynicism towards war - a view that carried over into the writings of the "Lost Generation" of 1920s literary figures such as Ernest Hemingway (*A Farewell to Arms*) and Erich Maria Remarque (*All Quiet on the Western Front*). The old order collapsed, from the Hapsburg Empire to the Romanov dynasty. The frenetic Jazz Age ushered in new fashion, new music, and a new culture. Nothing would be the same again, as the past 100 years have shown.

An American on the Western Front

Alan Seeger, a Harvard-educated poet and admirer of French culture, volunteered to fight for the France he came to love in 1914. He was killed on the Western front at Belloy-en-Santerre, France, in July 1916. The following excerpt is from a letter to a friend written on May 19th, 1916. From Letters and Diary of Alan Seeger, *New York: Charles Scribner's Sons, 1917, pp. 196-197.*

After a delightful month in Biarritz and another in Paris, I came back here the first of the month. I had really had such a good time, as I say, that I returned quite light-hearted… The sector was the quietest I had seen and one of great beauty, in the depths of the spring forest. Life here, in spite of the hard work, seemed no more than camping out and war only another way of spending the summer agreeably. These bright impressions, however, received a terrible shock yesterday and as I am still under the emotion of it, I will describe it to you.

With the warm weather we had left the underground proofs and pitched little shelter tents under the trees, where we slept or rested between the hours of guard. The dugouts were too hot and dirty and the sector seemed so calm that there was no danger. There were daily artillery duels, but battery sought battery and we were never troubled. Yesterday morning, however, a German aeroplane came over our lines. The cannonade was violent all day, but no one pays attention to that and most of us were lying down…when suddenly *whizz-bang! whizz-bang!* A terrible rafale of shrapnel began bursting right in our midst. Rush for the abris. But that there were victims was inevitable. Moans from outside. Cries to lend a hand. A sergeant and seven men had been touched. The most serious case was Corporal Colette, a splendid fellow whom everyone liked. They took him away on a litter, but he died before reaching the ambulance. Havoc in our little camp that had been so peaceful. Air full of dust and smell of powder, ground littered with leaves and branches, tents, clothes, equipment, riddled with holes, smashed and trailed with blood. Naturally since then we have had to come back to the bombproofs, where deep underground, we live in holes like those I remember pictured in our old natural histories, that show a gopher, an owl and a snake living happily together in the same burrow. Here it is men, rats, and vermin.

This is a typical episode of our life here on the front. It happens quickly and is quickly forgotten. Life is so cheap here.

1916 - Trenches at the Somme

Animals in the Great War

New technologies in World War I changed the way war was fought; among other things, this was the last war in which animals played a major role. Some animals served as mascots: some English regiments, for example, adopted golden eagles, some Welsh units employed goats, and black bears accompanied some Canadians. But while these animals served mostly as morale boosters for fighting men, others shared the same dangers as the men they served. Horses transported supplies and equipment through mud up to their knees. Dogs guarded prisoners of war, served as guides for those blinded during battle, and carried messages over dangerous terrain. Pigeons, too, carried messages over hostile terrain. Camels, oxen, donkeys and mules transported heavy artillery, oftentimes where travel was difficult and dangerous. As a consequence, animals were *Cont'd* often placed in some of the most dangerous environments.

Stories abound of deeds and acts of heroism made by animals. The French dog Satan "a mongrel by birth and thoroughbred by nature," saved an entire village and its garrison when he darted through German lines, wounded and without use of one leg, delivered a message and two carrier pigeons to boot. In another example, the American homing pigeon "Cher Ami" delivered twelve messages at the battle of Verdun and lost a leg successfully delivering a message during a battle in the Argonne Forest.

In the aftermath of the war, writer and photographer Ernest Baynes conducted a study of the many contributions made by animals during hostilities. Baynes estimated that some 8,000,000 horses alone died during the conflict. Many animals died from wounds received in battle and while transporting supplies and equipment. Others perished from exposure and disease. Nonetheless their contributions were significant to the fighting men of all armies.

Books Against War

In the aftermath of World War I, there were many works published that dealt with war. Some affirmed the need for, and morality of, war as a tool to create and protect democracy; one such, Willa Cather's *One of Our Own*, won the Pulitzer in 1923. But there was also an emerging body of literature that questioned the making of war and mocked the chivalry with which many writers glorified war. Instead of couching the brutality of war in terms of gallantry and heroic death, these younger writers saw only the irrationality and absurdity of war, and adamantly questioned military authority.

Works by such English writers as Robert Graves, Edmund Blunden, and Siegfried Sassoon, French writers such as Ronald Dorgeles and Henri Barbusse, Americans such as John Dos Passos, Malcolm Cowley, Thomas Boyd, E. E. Cummings, William March and William Faulkner, and even German writers Ludwig Renn, Arnold Zweig and Erich Maria Remarque with his *All Quiet on the Western Front*, called attention to the horrors of war, attacked the bankruptcy of war making or renounced war altogether.

Discussion Topics

1) Think of the new weapons technologies available in World War I. How do you think they affected the common footsoldier? Consider what you know of other, earlier wars. How do you think World War I was different? How do you think it was similar?

2) Read some of the poetry composed by the soldiers in the trenches of World War I. Why do you think the soldiers wrote this poetry? Describe how you think some of them were feeling when they were writing it. Do you think poetry is a good medium for expressing the horrors of war? Why? Why not?

3) Imagine it is May 1916. You are a friend of Alan Seeger, who wrote the letter that is excerpted on page 99. You receive his letter in the post one day. Describe how you would feel upon reading this. Write a letter to reply to him on the front lines with.

4) Do you think the generals and "higher-ups" of World War I were mostly to blame for the seemingly pointless deaths of so many soldiers? Explain your answer.

5) You are a soldier on the Western Front. Write a diary entry for an ordinary day in the trenches.

6) The Treaty of Versailles, which was issued against Germany by the powers that won World War I (France, Britain, Italy and the USA), can be considered as particularly harsh and unfair. It forced Germany to accept the full blame for the war and limited its armies for decades to come. Do you consider it overly unfair? Why? Why not?